Marriage and the Church's Task

The Report of the General Synod Marriage Commission

CIO PUBLISHING, Church House, Dean's Yard, London SW1

ISBN 0 7151 3684 4

GS 363

Published for the General Synod by the Church Information Office
1978

Printed in England by The Friary Press Limited, Dorchester, Dorset
and London

CONTENTS

The Commission

The Marriage Commission was set up by the Archbishops of Canterbury and York in October 1975 with the following terms of reference:

(1) To examine afresh the Christian doctrine of marriage and the marriage discipline of the Church of England, especially in the light of recent debates in the General Synod and elsewhere.

(2) To consider the understanding by contemporary people of the place of marriage as an institution.

(3) To report on the courses of action open to the Church in seeking to promote in contemporary society the Christian ideal of marriage as a life-long union between husband and wife.

The Bishop of Lichfield (the Rt Rev. Kenneth Skelton) was appointed Chairman of the Commission. The other members were:

The Ven. M. E. Adie
Mrs S. Aglionby
Mrs M. I. Allen
Canon Professor J. Atkinson
Canon Professor P. R. Baelz (Consultant)
Chancellor Sheila Cameron
Chancellor T. A. C. Coningsby
Mrs J. Dann
Mrs M. E. R. Holmes
The Very Rev. B. D. Jackson
Professor Kathleen Jones
Canon Barnabas Lindars SSF
Mr J. R. Lucas
Dr K. Soddy
The Rev. M. G. Whittock
Dr H. Morgan Williams

Mr W. D. Pattinson (Secretary-General) and Mr G. S. Ecclestone (Secretary of the Board for Social Responsibility) advised and assisted the Commission throughout its work. Mr Ecclestone also played a major part in the final drafting of the Report.

Mr Ecclestone aslo played a major part in the final drafting of the Report.

Mr B. J. T. Hanson (Legal Adviser to the General Synod) advised on a number of legal matters.

Mr D. J. B. Long (until September 1977) and Mr J. D. Hebblethwaite (in the final phase of the work) acted as secretaries to the Commission.

The Commission met for the first time on 21st October 1975; it subsequently met on 18 occasions, 12 of them being residential. It agreed to the present report on 11th February 1978.

1
Ten Years of Debate

1. This report is about marriage, and ways of promoting in our society the Christian understanding of marriage. It is also a report about divorce and marriage after divorce. It has been produced in response to a judgement that the Church of England's continuing witness in society to the importance of stable marriages and family life required at this time a fresh assessment of the Christian doctrine of marriage. Christian faithfulness calls for an equal sensitivity to what God is saying to us through the Bible, the Christian tradition and the life of the Church, and to what he is saying to us through the exigencies of human life, in this context the changing character of marriage as men and women encounter and live it. The authors of this report trust that it will assist the Church as it seeks to determine what that faithfulness requires.

2. For some ten years the Church has been engaged in keen debate over its understanding of the Christian doctrine of marriage and its implications for the strengthening of marriage as an institution, for the support of individuals and their marriages and for the pastoral care of those whose marriages fail. One reason for that debate has been a widespread dissatisfaction with the Church's existing discipline of marriage, and in particular with its rule that no divorced person who has a former partner still living may have a subsequent marriage solemnised in church. Against this background the Convocation of Canterbury in 1967 called for the preparation of a statement on the Christian doctrine of marriage. In 1968, the then Archbishop of Canterbury entrusted that task to a Commission under the Chairmanship of Canon Howard Root, Professor of Theology at Southampton University. In 1970, while the Commission was still sitting, the subject was debated by the Church Assembly at its final sessions. At about the same time, a Joint Committee of the Convocations was established to confer with the Commission. In 1971 the Root Commission published its report, *Marriage, Divorce and the Church*.[1] Between February 1972 and November 1974, the Root

---

[1] SPCK, 1971.

Report was debated by the General Synod on three separate occasions before its key proposals were rejected. In November 1974, the General Synod carried a motion calling for a fresh enquiry—and, as a result, the present Commission was set up. Throughout the whole period, and especially since the publication of the Root Report, the question of marriage and the Church's marriage discipline has been widely discussed up and down the country, and outside as well as inside the Church.

3. This decade of debate contrasts sharply with the confidence of the Church in the rightness of its marriage discipline during the five or six decades which preceded it. From the beginning of the present century the weight of Church opinion was opposed to any extension of the grounds for divorce beyond those sanctioned by Parliament in 1857. During the same period opposition to the marriage of divorced people in church stiffened, and was expressed in resolutions of the Convocations in 1938. This hardening of attitudes within the Church of England was echoed in the resolutions of successive Lambeth Conferences of Anglican bishops.

4. One expression of the state of Church opinion during this period can be seen in a pamphlet published in 1955 by Archbishop Fisher.[1] He summarised matters thus:

> The attitude of the Church of England, shortly put, is:
> (a) No marriage in church of any divorced person with a partner still living, since the solemnising of a marriage is a formal and official act of the Church, and the Church must not give its official recognition to a marriage which (for whatever cause) falls below our Lord's definition of what marriage is.
> (b) But the relation of such people to the Church or their admission to communion is another matter, one of pastoral care for the sinner, and properly a matter of pastoral discretion.

5. In 1957 the Convocation of Canterbury restated its opposition to the remarriage of divorced persons in church in new resolutions, which were declared to be an Act of Convocation possessing moral, though not legal, authority. Since these resolutions, together with the 1938 resolutions of the Convocation of York, state the official practice of the Church of England at the present time, we reproduce them in full:

> *Regulations Concerning Marriage and Divorce*
> 1 That this House reaffirms the following four Resolutions of 1938, and

[1]*Problems of Marriage and Divorce*, SPCK, 1955.

2

in place of Resolution 5 then provisionally adopted by the Upper House substitutes Resolution 2(A) below, which restates the procedure generally followed since 1938.

(1) That this House affirms that according to God's will, declared by Our Lord, marriage is in its true principle a personal union, for better or for worse, of one man with one woman, exclusive of all others on either side, and indissoluble save by death.

(2) That this House also affirms as a consequence that remarriage after divorce during the lifetime of a former partner always involves a departure from the true principle of marriage as declared by our Lord.

(3) That in order to maintain the principle of lifelong obligation which is inherent in every legally contracted marriage and is expressed in the plainest terms in the Marriage Service, the Church should not allow the use of that Service in the case of anyone who has a former partner still living.

(4) That while affirming its adherence to our Lord's principle and standard of marriage as stated in the first and second of the above resolutions, this House recognises that the actual discipline of particular Christian Communions in this matter has varied widely from time to time and place to place, and holds that the Church of England is competent to enact such a discipline of its own in regard to marriage as may from time to time appear most salutary and efficacious.

2(A) Recognising that the Church's pastoral care for all people includes those who during the lifetime of a former partner contract a second union, this House approves the following pastoral regulations as being the most salutary in present circumstances:

(a) When two persons have contracted a marriage in civil law during the lifetime of a former partner of either of them, and either or both desire to be baptised or confirmed or to partake of the Holy Communion, the incumbent or other priest having the cure of their souls shall refer the case to the Bishop of the diocese, with such information as he has and such recommendations as he may desire to make.

(b) The Bishop in considering the case shall give due weight to the preservation of the Church's witness to Our Lord's standard of marriage and to the pastoral care of those who have departed from it.

(c) If the Bishop is satisfied that the parties concerned are in good faith and that their receiving of the Sacraments would be for the good of their souls and ought not to be a cause of offence to the Church, he shall signify his approval thereof both to the priest and to the party or parties concerned: this approval shall be given in writing and shall be accepted as authoritative both in the particular diocese and in all other dioceses of the province.

2(B) No public Service shall be held for those who have contracted a civil marriage after divorce. It is not within the competence of the Convocations to lay down what private prayers the curate in the exercise of his pastoral Ministry may say with the persons concerned, or to issue regulations as to where or when these prayers shall be said.

2(C) Recognising that pastoral care may well avert the danger if it comes into play before legal proceedings have been started, this House urges all clergy in their preparation of couples for marriage to tell them, both for their own sakes and for that of their friends, that the good offices of the clergy are always available.

THE ROOT COMMISSION

6. The Church of England found itself, by the 1960s, to be the most rigorist of all Churches in its pastoral practice in matrimonial cases. Increasingly, Anglican provinces overseas were beginning to allow remarriage after divorce, subject to safeguards. The Orthodox and the Reformed Churches had long allowed remarriage in certain cases at least. And the Roman Catholic Church, while officially and formally rigorist, was responding to changing pastoral needs by enlarging the scope of its concept of nullity. Within the Church of England, voices were heard questioning the position which the Convocations had adopted. Meanwhile, in the report entitled *Putting Asunder,* a group appointed by the then Archbishop of Canterbury had made an important contribution to the reformation of the State's law of divorce by proposing that henceforward the sole grounds for divorce in the public law of England should be the irretrievable breakdown of marriage.[1] Against this background the Root Commission appointed in 1968 set about producing (as they said in their report *Marriage, Divorce and the Church*) a 'plain and authoritative statement of the Christian teaching on marriage' which would take into account the 'secular realities of marriage and divorce as these are now known'—realities which, through personal experience, were leading Christian men and women to decide in good conscience to divorce and later to remarry.

7. The Commission approached their task by first exploring the Christian understanding of the nature of marriage. Marriage as a relationship between persons they saw as meeting certain fundamental needs, and requiring for its fullness the elements of exclusiveness, commitment and permanence. They drew attention to the interest society has in marriage as an institution, and the

[1]SPCK, 1966.

4

expression of that interest in statutory regulation of marriages and divorce as well as in other ways. In their review of the biblical sources of Christian understanding the Commission emphasised that Jesus had taught that 'in the purposes of God marriage was meant to be permanent'.[1] At the same time, while his teaching was 'vigorous and demanding' in its implications (since Jesus was concerned to point to the true nature of marriage), his words were not to be taken as legislation. As such, the Commission argued, the Church was free to draw up its own rules to meet the situation where a couple fail to meet the demands of Jesus' teaching, and a marriage dies.

8.   Turning to the immediate situation in the Church of England, the Root Commission said:

> There are, as we have seen, ecclesiastical regulations which discourage a second marriage of divorced persons from being solemnised in church. Unquestionably such regulations should remain in being if the moral consensus of Christian people in the Church of England requires it. But the question must be asked whether there is this moral consensus. It is not for the Commission to attempt to determine the answer to this question; but there is sufficient evidence to oblige us to raise this question and others which follow from it. Is there a growing consensus among Christian people, both clerical and lay, first, that some marriages, however well-intentioned, do break down; secondly, that some divorced partners enter into new unions in good faith and that some of these new unions show such evident features of stability, complementarity, fruitfulness, and growth as to make them comparable with satisfactory first marriages; and thirdly, that Christian congregations are not scandalised, in the theological sense of the word, by the presence of such persons in their midst or by their participation in the Holy Communion? If an affirmative answer is given to these questions, then we are bound to raise the question that naturally follows from such an answer. Is there also a growing moral consensus that such persons, with due safeguards, may properly have their marriages solemnised according to the rites of the Church? Indeed, it may well turn out on inquiry that a moral judgement on this matter has already formed itself within the Church of England, as it has in some other Churches of the Anglican Communion, in the belief that remarriage in church would be not a weakening but a strengthening of marriage. It is possible that those who say that to remarry in church would cause offence to the Christian conscience may find that failure to do so causes greater offence.[2]

9.   The Commission went on to sketch the conditions on which it would be appropriate to allow second or subsequent marriages to be

---

[1] *Op. cit.*, p. 94.
[2] *Op. cit.*, p. 71-2.

solemnised in church. There would need, first, to be discreet enquiries regarding the discharge of obligations arising from the previous marriage, into the attitudes of the persons seeking to marry afresh, and as to their intention that the new marriage would be permanent. The Commission did not make specific proposals about the procedures to be followed. But they appeared to be envisaging that enquiries would be undertaken by or on behalf of the bishop. At the same time, the right which the incumbent has had in statute law to marry divorced persons in church ever since 1857—and which existing ecclestiastical regulations seek to dissuade him from exercising—would remain. In other words, whatever the diocesan advice might be, there would be an ultimate discretion exercised by the parish priest.

10. The Commission's findings amounted to a direct challenge to the Church's pastoral practice as regards the marriage of divorced people in church, and to the theological basis on which that practice rested. They pointed out that it would be for the General Synod formally to test opinion to determine whether a consensus in favour of change existed; if such a consensus were found to exist 'then it would be the duty of the Bishops-in-Synod to determine whether this consensus is theologically well-founded'.[1] The Commission declared it as their unanimous view that there *was* a sound theological base for such a change.

11. Many people welcomed the Root Report. But it fared poorly in the General Synod, where a substantial body of members were unsympathetic to it from its first appearance there.[2] At the end of the first debate (February 1972) a motion which would have commended the Report for study in the dioceses was amended to make clear that the views did not have the backing of a majority of the General Synod. Many observers felt that the second debate (in November 1973) showed clearly enough that the key proposal in the Report was unacceptable to a majority in the Synod. But certain technicalities in the course of that debate gave supporters of the Root proposals ground for pressing for a further debate. This, when it came, showed clearly and unmistakably that the General Synod was not to be persuaded to test opinion on the Root proposals.

---

[1] *Op. cit.*, p. 72.
[2] For a full report of the debates see the *Report of Proceedings* of the General Synod:
February group of sessions 1972 Vol. 3. No. 1, pages 75-116. November group of sessions 1973 Vol. 4. No. 3, pages 727-780. November group of sessions 1974 Vol. 5. No. 3, pages 808-837.

12. A study of the three Synod debates shows certain threads running throughout, with others emerging only in the second and third debates. There was opposition from some members who rejected the possibility of divorce on theological grounds; from these and others came criticism of the theological and biblical sections of the Report and its Appendices. There was a feeling that to allow second marriages in church would weaken the effectiveness of the Church's witness to the Christian ideal, since the marriage of divorcees would involve people in taking lifelong vows twice. There was dislike of the concept of consensus: a course of action, it was argued, was right or wrong, and its rightness did not depend on the existence of a consensus. There was anxiety about the exposed position in which the Report seemed to place the parish priest; he would be able to take advice concerning the desirability of allowing remarriage in a particular case, but the final decision would be his. Whatever the intrinsic merits of their proposals, there was anxiety about the wisdom of the course recommended by the Commission in a situation in which the divorce rate was continuing to rise significantly.

13. By the time of the third debate, this last consideration loomed ever larger, with another issue closely linked with it. The Divorce Reform Act 1969 came into operation on 1st January 1971. In that Act Parliament—following up some of the proposals in *Putting Asunder*—had abolished the concept of the matrimonial offence, substituting as the sole ground for divorce the irretrievable breakdown of the marriage. Two features in particular of the Act had attracted criticism. It was possible to establish breakdown by evidence that the couple had lived apart for two years and that both partners agreed to seek a divorce. Breakdown could also be established on evidence of five years' separation, even if one partner was opposed to the divorce. For the first time in England, it appeared, a 'blameless' person could be divorced against his or her will. Reflecting on the significance of these legal changes, some people had begun to argue that they represented a move by the State to a concept of marriage which might be consistent with current secular attitudes to marriage but which could no longer be said to be consistent with Christian principles. Thus by 1974 the ground of debate in the Synod had broadened. The theological argument remained—some people were clearly dissatisfied with the Root Commission's findings. But a fresh look, it was argued, should include consideration of a range of major social and legal issues scarcely touched upon in the Root

Report. The Church needed, it was said, to look, as a matter of urgency, at its relationship in these matters with the wider community—to look at the effects of the 1969 changes in the law, to look at the way those changes—and marriage generally—are being understood in the community in which we live. It needed to ask whether in respect of marriage there was still sufficient agreement between Church and State, to justify the Church regarding civil marriage as marriage in the Christian understanding, or whether the divergence between the two standards was such that Church and State should from now on each set its own standards and formulate its own procedures.

14. These various considerations were distilled in the resolution agreed by the General Synod at the end of the 1974 debate, namely:

That this Synod
(i) notes with concern the change in understanding of the nature of marriage expressed in the Divorce Reform Act 1969,
(ii) is therefore of the opinion that further consideration of proposals for the remarriage of divorced persons in church should be deferred until there has been a fresh examination of the Christian doctrine of marriage and of marriage discipline in the Church of England, and
(iii) asks the Presidents and the Standing Committee to arrange for this examination, so that the General Synod and diocesan synods can at an early date give further consideration to these important issues.

OUR TASK

15. The terms of reference given to us by the Presidents and the Standing Committee (see p. v above) reflect the range of concerns expressed in the 1974 debate and in the motion carried at its conclusion. We were asked to consider afresh the Christian doctrine of marriage and the marriage discipline of the Church of England, taking account of recent debates in the Synod—that is, of the debates on the Root Commission's Report: this task requires a theological judgement from us, as well as a consideration of the appropriateness of that discipline to the present situation. We were also asked to consider the understanding by contemporary people of marriage as an institution—to consider how the community (through the law and in other ways) regards marriage, and how that understanding is reflected in the state of marriage today. Finally, we were asked, in the light of all this, to report on the courses of action open to the Church in commending to people in our society the Christian understanding of marriage.

16. The task given to us, and its particular context, have shaped the character of our Report. We first look at the contemporary experience and understanding of marriage and deal with the specific legal issues raised in debates in the General Synod. We then review the theological evidence and indicate what in our judgement can be said concerning the Christian doctrine of marriage. In the light of both these types of evidence we consider the theological and moral implications of changes in the institution of marriage in our society, and the consequences of these for the Church's pastoral practice and its duty in society. We deal at this point not only with the central questions of remarriage in church but also with detailed matters relating to the marriage of the unbaptised, and the position of ordinands and clergy who marry after divorce. We end the Report with our Recommendations as to the action to be taken. We deal in a number of Appendices with certain incidental matters which arose in our work, and also with certain matters which require fuller treatment than there is room for in the main text of our Report. The Appendices represent in the main contributions by particular members of the Commission, though they have been discussed by the Commission and amended in the light of that discussion. They do not, therefore, commit the Commission as the main body of the report does.

17. It is perhaps important that we should point to certain things which we have *not* done. The starting point of our Report was a response to the debates held in the Synod and elsewhere in the Church between 1972 and 1974. There was therefore no need to go in any detail over the ground traversed by the Root Commission where, as it seems, their findings are not in issue. But if in the Report and Appendices we have not considered in detail, for example, the attitude or practice of other Provinces of the Anglican Communion or of the Orthodox Churches, this does not mean that we have been unmindful of their relevance to our enquiry.

2
The Institution of Marriage

'. . . to consider the understanding by contemporary people of the place of marriage as an institution . . .'

18.   The relationship which a man and a woman enter on their wedding day is both unique to them and shared with countless others in space and time. It is the most intimate and lasting encounter with another person which most of us ever have; it is also, in almost every society we know, a 'public' relationship, regulated by law and requiring for its validity some form of public recognition. Marriage is not a simple, unitary concept. It is a portmanteau of legal, theological, psychological, social and economic concepts which vary in emphasis and interpretation over time and between societies, and also between groups and individuals within a given society. It is a compound of hopes and expectations, never quite the same for one couple and the next.

19.   In our society, as in many others, the relationship between a husband and wife is treated as in the main privileged and private. There are few external requirements which constrain the relationship in specific directions. Its character is likely therefore to be influenced mainly by the way in which the couple themselves respond to circumstances and social attitudes. In a period of rapid social and economic change, it is to be expected that interest will be focused on the differences between marriage today and in the past; but it is useful to remember that marriage also represents a way by which people can *manage* change, both in their social environment and within themselves. Patterns of married life are influenced by wider social change, but the institution of marriage has a contribution to make to social and personal stability.

20.   One of our early tasks was to consider how this part of our terms of reference should be approached. Some members of the Commission were initially in favour of a social survey, since they felt that this would produce the kind of hard evidence needed. After considerable

discussion, we rejected this possibility for a number of reasons. The most obvious of these were the problems of cost and time. Valid social surveys require a great deal of testing and piloting, the careful construction of a sample population, the framing of a questionnaire in terms which are easily comprehensible to all sections of society, and which are sufficiently neutral not to suggest the form which the answer ought to take, extensive interviewing, and computer analysis. These essentially technical tasks were beyond our resources and the time-scale of our enquiry. We were also doubtful about the usefulness of results, even if it had been possible to carry out survey work with full scientific rigour. While it would have been possible to gather hard evidence about the number of marriages and divorces, the number of children involved in divorces, and the preference of couples for marriage ceremonies of different types, such material is already available from Government statistical sources. Questions about people's views on marriage in general are of a different order. Responses may be based on varying degrees of agreement or indifference, experience or inexperience, and differing assumptions and prejudices, of which survey methods tell us little or nothing. A survey 'about marriage' would cover very wide areas of human concern—patterns of sexual behaviour, assumptions about the roles of men and women in society, the nature of family life, and many more—which are not reducible to simple question form, and do not admit of simple, clear-cut answers.

21. We were convinced that a study of contemporary understanding, to be of any real value, must be interpretative rather than quantitative. It must make some assessment of changes taking place, and include some estimate of whether phenomena to be observed at one point in time are a matter of passing fashion, or expressions of more fundamental and long-term changes in human patterns of conduct. What is 'contemporary' at the time of writing soon dates unless it is seen to have its roots in the past and its fruition in the future. Time needs to be handled in chunks rather than in fragments if we are to understand the meaning of change.

22. We were concerned also to consider how far such changes as we observed could be said to have moral and theological implications, and this was beyond the scope of any social survey. The issue touches on one of the central problems of religous belief and practice: in what respects is changing social behaviour a matter of failing to preserve

11

traditional insights, a falling away from standards revealed to us in the Bible and the teaching of the Church? In what respects is it a matter of adaptation to changing conditions, neither better nor worse than what went before? In what respects is it the result of new insights, the Holy Spirit guiding us into greater understanding? The answers to these questions may not always be clear, but the questions must be asked.

23. We concluded that survey work, while it would lend a superficial air of credibility to our findings, was no substitute for the process of careful inquiry and judgement for which the Commission had been set up, and that our proper task was to study the evidence available rather than to attempt to create new evidence of our own. Our basic method has therefore been two-fold: we have studied the statistical evidence on marriage and divorce in our own society, and we have sought explanations for the changes which we have observed.

STATISTICS ON MARRIAGE AND DIVORCE[1]

24. In the 1960s, there seemed no doubt about the popularity of marriage as an institution. There was a steady upward trend in the number of marriages from a 1961 figure of 347,000 to 416,000 in 1970. The 1971 figure was somewhat lower, but in 1972 a peak figure of 426,000 was reached. Since then, the trend has been downward. The 1975 total of 381,000 was 11 per cent fewer than that of 1972.

25. These totals conceal differing trends in the numbers of first and subsequent marriages. The number of marriages where both partners were marrying for the first time has fallen every year since 1970, by a greater amount than can be accounted for by the drop in the numbers of single people of marriageable age. The marriage of the divorced has increased sharply, the numbers of divorced people marrying nearly doubling in the same period.

26. In 1961, there were 25,000 divorces. The number rose steadily year by year to 58,000 in 1970. The Divorce Reform Act 1969 became effective on 1st January 1971, and the 1972 figures reflected a sharp

---

[1]Figures in this chapter and in other chapters of the Report are based on publications of the Office of Population Censuses and Surveys (OPCS), on an article by Mr Richard Leete of OPCS *(Population Trends 3,* Spring 1976) and on personal advice from Mr Leete which is gratefully acknowledged. Detailed statistical information is given in Appendix 1. Unless otherwise indicated, figures are for England and Wales.

increase to 119,000. Numbers of divorces have since remained high. In 1975, 121,000 divorces were made absolute, and 140,000 fresh petitions filed. The divorce rate now stands at over nine per thousand existing marriages: that is, almost one couple in a hundred obtains a divorce within a given year. This does not represent the whole of marriage breakdown, since some couples obtain a legal separation, and some take no legal action at all.

27.   There is some evidence that marriages contracted by young people may face a disproportionately high risk of breakdown. At present, in some 30 per cent of all first marriages, the bride is marrying before her twentieth birthday. A study of marriages taking place in 1958-9 indicated that marriages contracted by people under 20 were more than twice as likely to have been dissolved 15 years later than those contracted by people aged between 20 and 24.[1]

28.   The number of children involved annually in divorce proceedings has kept pace with the increase in divorce. In 1975, 145,000 children under the age of 16 were involved in divorce proceedings, of whom nearly a quarter were under the age of five.

29.   This picture of changing patterns of marriage and divorce has led to widespread fears about the breakdown of marriage as an institution, and considerable publicity has been given by press and television to the development of alternative forms of sexual and domestic behaviour—trial marriage, group living, so-called 'open marriage' and others. Much of this caters for a public taste for sensation. Adultery is news, fidelity is not. Nevertheless, there has been a legitimate public concern with the effects of marriage breakdown on the stability of society.

30.   Attempts to find reasons for the lower number of marriages or the striking increase in divorce, or to predict whether either will continue, must at present be tentative. There is no simple pattern of cause and effect, and while it is possible to suggest some reasons for the changes currently observed, it is too early to say which are exerting the greatest effect, or what impact they will have over time. Short-term runs of statistics are unreliable indicators. In order to interpret what is happening in the 1970s, we need at least a ten- or fifteen-year run: that is, we need statistics which will not be available until the late 1980s or the 1990s.

[1] R. Leete, art. cit., p. 6.

31.   One factor is the change in the law which occurred with the passing of the Divorce Reform Act 1969; but we need to distinguish two kinds of reference to 'the law'. One is to the actual words of a Public General Statute, as cited by lawyers; the other is to the way in which a statute is interpreted by the courts and applied in practice. Law derives its sanction from society through Parliament. It is shaped by social attitudes, and shapes them in turn.

32.   It became clear in the 1950s and 1960s that divorce no longer carried the social stigma formerly associated with it. One outcome of the changed climate of opinion (to which *Putting Asunder*, the report of the Archbishop's Group on the law of divorce, contributed) was the 1969 Act. The number of divorces was already increasing, partly in anticipation of the Act. After its implementation, the rise was even sharper; but we have no means of distinguishing between cases in which the marriage had virtually ceased to exist many years earlier, and cases in which the change in the law preceded (and perhaps made more likely) the breakdown of the marriage. Some at least of the couples who have sought divorce since the passing of the Act may have separated much earlier, and set up second households which it only then became possible to regularise. Divorce statistics tell us about the legal position of the couples involved, not about the human realities behind the figures. Knowledge of legal change diffuses slowly and unevenly, and people do not always act on it at once. We cannot yet say what proportion of the current number of divorces is 'a result of the Act' in the sense that the Act made regularisation of an existing situation possible, and what proportion is 'a result of the Act' in the sense that the Act affected social attitudes to marriage as an institution.

33.   Some publicity has been given to statements that there is now 'one divorce for every two marriages'. This view can be superficially supported by the figures: in 1975, there were 265,000 first marriages and 121,000 divorces, with 140,000 divorce petitions filed for the following year; but the figures cannot be accepted without qualification. The number of marriages in the late 1960s and the early 1970s was high because the age-groups in which most marriages occur (20-24 and 25-29) were large: these were the 'bulge' children of the post-war period, when birth-rates were unusually high. The present number of marriages is affected by the comparatively low birth-rates of the early 1950s. In addition, the Family Law Reform Act of 1969

14

enabled young people to marry at the age of 18 without parental consent, and a spate of teenage marriages followed. If these marriages were, so to speak, brought forward by legislative change, we could expect some decrease in the number of marriages in the ensuing years. It is also possible that some couples are now postponing marriage to a later age—though how far this is due to a harsher economic climate or to the increased social acceptability of unmarried households is difficult to say.

34.　The juxtaposition of marriage and divorce statistics for the same year is in any case misleading, since couples who seek divorce now were married some years earlier: the two sets of figures do not refer to the same people, and they reflect differing demographic and social pressures. The divorce figures in the mid-1970s reflect, *inter alia*, the higher number of marriages in the previous decade, and the risk attached to the teenage marriages of the earlier 1970s.

35.　There are, therefore, statistical grounds for doubting whether the changes in the figures for marriage and divorce are as alarming as they look at first sight. Only further statistical evidence will enable us to make more precise interpretations of changing trends.

36.　In 1965, 77 per cent of first marriages were by religious solemnisation, 51 per cent Anglican (i.e. according to the rites of the Church of England or the Church in Wales) and 26 per cent 'other' (i.e. according to the rites of the Roman Catholic Church or the Free Churches). By 1975, the overall figure for religious solemnisation had dropped to 68 per cent, 49 per cent Anglican and 19 per cent 'other'. The increase in the use of civil ceremonies may in part be explicable in terms of a decline in religious belief and practice. It may relate to a desire for simplicity and low costs, since a 'church wedding' is still often thought of as· a major social occasion of a traditional kind. It may, as the Registrar-General has suggested, relate to the increased attractiveness of register offices, where music and flowers are now often introduced to enhance the dignity of what was formerly often a very perfunctory occasion. All that can be said with certainty is that register office weddings have become marginally more popular with couples marrying for the first time, but that over two-thirds still seek a Christian marriage ceremony, and half seek an Anglican ceremony.

37.　Where one or both partners in a marriage have been pre-viously married and divorced, the position is very different. The great majority seek marriage in a register office—89 per cent in 1965, and 88 per cent in 1975. But the numbers of divorced people marrying are increasing sharply, and the numbers coming to the churches for marriage are increasing also. In 1975, the Roman Catholic Church conducted 666 marriages in which one party was divorced, and 32 in which both parties were divorced. The Free Churches (Methodist, Congregationalist, Baptist and United Reformed Churches) conducted 8,792 marriages in which one party was divorced and 1,668 in which both were divorced. The corresponding figures for Anglican ceremonies were, one party divorced: 411; both parties divorced: 65. Marriages by Anglican ceremony represented less than half of one per cent of all marriages involving divorced persons. The small numbers of second marriages after divorce taking place in Anglican churches reflects the operation of the Convocation Regulations (see para. 5.).

38. However cautious our approach to the statistics, we are left facing some harsh facts. Many marriages do break down. Many children have the experience of a broken home. Marriage after divorce is increasing rapidly, and is usually a secular ceremony. The problems have grown substantially more acute in recent years. We need to ask how the understanding of marriage has changed: what conditions militate against fidelity in marriage and stability in family life; and whether marriage, despite all the evidence of failure, is still a central institution in our society.

DEFINING MARRIAGE

39. We use the term 'marriage' to describe both the wedding ceremony and 'the state of holy matrimony'—that is, the partnership which husband and wife begin on their wedding day, and hope to live out through the years ahead. In former generations, the two meanings were practically synonymous, since the overwhelming majority of those who married stayed married. That is no longer the case, and the gradual decline of the terms 'to wed' and 'wedding' in connection with the marriage ceremony is to be regretted, because it obscures the distinction.

40. A further difficulty in discussion is that we use the term 'marriage' to describe a cluster of expectations about the relationship of a man and a woman. We expect it to be a loving relationship, based on mutual attraction and shared values; a sexual relationship, based

on physical attraction and shared physical satisfaction; a biological relationship, leading to the birth and nurture of children; a social relationship, involving the family of marriage in a network of wider family and community contacts; an economic relationship, based on a common domicile, the marital home, and a sharing of possessions and income. All this is formalised in a legal and institutional relationship involving public recognition and mutual contractual responsibilities. We expect this complex web of relationships to be exclusive, and to last throughout the joint lives of the partners.

41. This cluster of expectations describes an ideal of marriage which not all can attain. Most of us have known real-life marriages in which one or more of these attributes is not present. The social and economic context of marriage, and the expectations and motivations of the partners, have been subject to massive changes over time, particularly in recent years.

CHANGING PATTERNS OF MARRIAGE

42. Generalising about a relationship as intimate and personal as marriage is always difficult, and increasingly so in a period when traditional attitudes and modes of behaviour are questioned, and patterns of adjustment diversify; but a number of features in change can be identified. The duration of marriage has greatly increased for most couples, and the significance of child-bearing and child-rearing to the whole span of marriage has declined. The late Richard Titmuss, writing in the 1950s, pointed out that the mother of a working-class family in 1900 'could not expect to finish with the affairs of child care until she was in the middle fifties . . . the situation today is remarkably different . . . by the time the typical mother of today has virtually completed the cycle of motherhood, she still has practically half her total life expectancy to live.'[1] Thus the scale and character of the commitment to marriage have both altered.

43. The economic and social setting of the commitment has altered also. In predominantly rural societies such as we had in Britain before industrialisation, families are held together by the land. Young couples tend to bring up their children in the village, and often in the household, where their parents live. While there is considerable debate about the process of the decline of the extended family, it is

[1] R. M. Titmuss, *Essays on 'the Welfare State'*, Allen and Unwin, 1958, pp. 92-3.

clear that urbanisation has turned us into a race of industrial nomads, living for the most part in cities, and among strangers. Many young couples now lack the kind of day-to-day family support which was common in the past, and live out the vital years of early married life in comparative isolation. This bears particularly hardly on them when they start a family, though the combination of statutory health and social services with such means of self-help as baby-sitting groups and play-groups goes some way towards meeting their needs.

44. With the decline in extended family and established neighbourhood networks has gone a decline in patriarchal forms of authority, both as exercised by a father over his children and by a husband over his wife. The power of the male property-owner as head of the family has been increasingly eroded by the development of a society in which social and economic standing for both sexes and all adults are derived from income and the ability to borrow rather than from inheritance. The decline of vertical lines of authority is reflected in new patterns of family life, just as it is reflected in the development of parliamentary democracy, worker participation in industry, or the Church of England's own system of synodical government. Women and adult children have their own status as citizens, rather than deriving their economic and social status exclusively from the head of the household.

45. Traditionally, man and wife have had strongly differentiated and complementary roles, and the survival of the family depended on competent role fulfilment. The man provided for and protected his wife and children. The woman bore a child a year, brought up the children, and fed and clothed the whole family. Today, the economic battle for survival has moved decisively out of the home. It is expressed primarily in getting a job, earning money, and buying goods from the supermarket.

46. Women have been freed from the annual cycle of child-bearing by the development of reliable and readily available contraceptives, and planned families, commonly of two or three children, have become the norm. Automation has removed many of the limitations on women's employment relating to physical strength, since the gender of the hand that presses the button is irrelevant. The result of these changes has been more than a matter of 'equality for women'. It has meant a new analysis of gender-roles for both sexes which is at once challenging and disturbing.

47.   One major consideration in the changed economic and social relationship of the sexes is the reversal of the traditional numerical balance between them. We are used to thinking in terms of 'excess women'—a biological surplus which provides for both married home-makers who do not undertake paid employment, and unmarried female workers; but there are now more males than females in all age-groups up to the age of 45. This change seems to be due largely to improvements in obstetric and maternal care, and to better education for mothers and nutrition of their children. More males than females have always been conceived, but a higher rate of male foetal deaths, and neonatal and infant mortality has kept down the male population, while war reduced it still further in young adulthood. The full social effects of the change have yet to be analysed; but it clearly increases the pressure for women to enter employment, and for men to undertake what were formerly regarded as women's tasks. Men are now entering such traditionally feminine occupations as social work, nursing and primary school teaching. In the home, there is often a new appraisal of the tasks of bread-winning and home-making when both partners work.

48.   There are now three main patterns of economic relationships within marriage in western society.[1] One is the traditional pattern in which the husband is the bread-winner and the wife the home-maker. Increasingly, this is being restricted to the more prosperous sections of society, to couples with large families, and to those who deliberately accept a limited income for the sake of a way of life which they wish to maintain. The second, now more common, pattern is one in which the wife undertakes paid employment before marriage and perhaps for some years after, reverts to the role of full-time home-maker while the children are dependent, and then goes back to paid work in her late thirties or forties. The third is the pattern in which both sexes share the tasks of earning and home-making throughout their married life until the age of retirement, the woman taking short periods of leave for childbirth. It seems likely that all three patterns will continue. Husbands and wives will make their own decisions about such fundamental concerns in the light of their economic circumstances and their understanding of what marriage means to them.

---

[1]E. Dahlström, *The Changing Roles of Men and Women,* tr. Gunilla and Steven Anderson, Beacon Press, Boston, Mass. 1971.

49.   In the past few years, there have been new developments which affect the marriage relationship in its most personal aspects: a much greater explicitness about sexual practicies; wide public acceptance of commercially-promoted pornographic books and films; simple, legal and relatively safe abortion. The link between sex and marriage has been loosened, and young people are affected by this long before they reach the age of marriage. Many want to know quite seriously what arguments are left against promiscuity now that the risk of unwanted pregnancies has been virtually removed, and chastity is apparently devalued. For many, sexual experience probably comes much earlier than in the past. The discovery that it involves human relationships, and the grief when such relationships fail, can be acute and psychologically damaging. But there are signs of hope in this recognition. With the risk of pregnancy removed, young people are looking carefully at the quality of their relationships, realising that sex is important, but not all-important. Having learnt that sex without love does not make for lifelong happiness, they may avoid the mistakes of some of their 'elders and betters'.

THE LOSS OF A GOLDEN AGE?
50.   The developments we have outlined have brought new freedom to individuals, but little guidance in how to use it. Peter Laslett's *The World We Have Lost*[1] gives a vivid picture of the small-scale, pastoral world of the pre-industrial period, but warns us against an uncritical nostalgia for the past. That world had its own stresses and uncertainties—often a struggle for sheer physical survival in the face of disease, hunger and war. Professor Donald MacRae, in his appendix to *Putting Asunder*,[2] points out that an appeal to a mythical 'golden age' when human relations or societal values were very much better than they are now is profoundly un-historical—though the myth will continue to be employed because it serves to legitimise specific traditional ideas which its advocates wish to maintain.

51.   Given the insecurity and uncertainty engendered by rapidly-accelerating social change, the new economic, social and psychological stresses, it is understandable that there should be a tendency to gild the features of pre-industrial society. The shift from

[1]P. Laslett, *The World We Have Lost*, Methuen, 2nd edition, 1971.
[2]D. MacRae, Appendix F to *Putting Asunder*, SPCK, 1966.

village-based societies to the kind of mass, commercially-oriented society in which we live today has occupied many historians and sociologists in the search for explanation, but there is general agreement that industrialisation has created one of the major discontinuities in human history. Even if we wished to do so, we cannot put the clock back. A long period of changing circumstances and changing values stands between us and the societies from which our traditional models of married life are derived. Each period of history has its own problems, its own potential for good or evil. Our task is not to reach back to an unattainable past, but to work out the moral implications of the conditions of our own day.

THE SOCIOLOGICAL UNDERSTANDING OF MARRIAGE

52. Though patterns of married life are diversifying, we do not believe that the institution of marriage is likely to decline. There is increasing recognition that, though it is possible to avoid the biological consequences of pre-marital and extra-marital relationships in unwanted pregnancies, the psychological consequences in terms of damaged personal identity when temporary relationships fail can be serious and long-lasting. Sociologists have shown little interest in the husband-wife relationship until recent years, the classic view being that of Westermarck, who held that 'the family is not rooted in marriage, but marriage is rooted in the family'.[1] The marital relationship was seen as significant only insofar as it created the stable and protective environment which the human young needed until they were old enough to care for themselves.

53. In the past few years, there has been a new interest in the mutual relationship of husband and wife as the basis of family interaction and family stability. The ways in which the couple acquire new status, new roles, and undertake new tasks together has been described and analysed.[2] One influential study has argued that the family is rooted in marriage, describing marriage as a 'nomos-building instrumentality'—that is, a means of building a small private society in which the couple, and later their children, can experience and explain life to each other. 'It is in marriage that the

---

[1]E. Westermarck, *The History of Human Marriage*, Macmillan, 1921, p. 22.
[2]See, e.g. R. O. Blood and D. M. Wolfe, *Husbands and Wives: The Dynamics of Married Living*, Collier-Macmillan, 1960; E. Bott, *Family and Social Network*, Tavistock Publications, 1971.

21

individual will seek power, intelligibility and quite literally a name—the apparent power to fashion a world, however Lilliputian, which will reflect his own being'. The authors conclude: 'Whether one legitimates one's maritally constructed reality in terms of "mental health" or of "the sacrament of marriage" is today left largely to free consumer preference, but it is indicative of a new overall universe of discourse that it is possible to do both at the same time.'[1]

54. If marriage has to fulfil these high expectations, the emphasis on the relationship between husband and wife, no longer buttressed by clear-cut social roles, strong extended family networks and economic pressures which often made the splitting up of the marital home unthinkable, demands a great deal of them. The institution of marriage now stands or falls on the quality of the interpersonal relationship between the couple. The potential for richness of personal fulfilment may be greater: the risk of failure is certainly greater, and the price of failure may be high. Marriage breakdown may mean not only the loss of a sexual partner and companion, but the destruction of a shared universe of meaning and understanding.

THE LAW ON MARRIAGE AND DIVORCE

55. The new emphasis on the primacy of personal relationships in marriage has been reflected in the law. Though we shall argue that the Divorce Reform Act of 1969 has not in any material way altered the law's understanding of what is required of a valid marriage, it is apparent that the English divorce law, like jurisdictions elsewhere in the world, has responded to a shift of understanding of what marriage means. The introduction into the law of the principle of marital breakdown indicates a primary concern for the emotional compatibility of the couple ('The petitioner finds it intolerable to live with the respondent'), and a movement away from the view that divorce is a remedy available to a wronged spouse. In the sections which follow, we describe briefly the major features of present English law on marriage and divorce; further information is given in Appendix 7.

---

[1]P. Berger and H. Keller, 'Marriage and the Construction of Reality' in H. P. Dreitzel (ed.) *Recent Sociology No. 2,* Collier-Macmillan 1970; reprinted in R. L. Coser (ed.) *The Family: its Structures and Functions,* Macmillan, 1974.

Marriage

56. Marriage in English law has been defined as 'the voluntary union for life of one man and one woman to the exclusion of all others'.[1] Marriage, that is, must in its inception be for life. If the union entered upon were for a term less than life, English law would not recognise it as a marriage at all.[2] There can therefore be no such thing as a trial or temporary marriage.

57. While the act of marrying has features analogous to entry upon a contract in other circumstances, the state of *being* married is not a contractual relationship but a 'status'.

> Marriage is the fulfilment of a contract satisfied by the solemnisation of the marriage, but marriage directly it exists creates by law a relation between the parties and what is called a status of each. The status of an individual used as a legal term means the legal position of the individual in or with regard to the rest of a community. That relation between the parties, and that status of each of them with regard to the community, which are constituted upon marriage are not imposed or defined by contract or agreement but by law.[3]

58. It is also a fundamental feature of the English law on marriage that it applies to all persons living in England. Anyone wishing to enter into a marriage in this country can contract only a monogamous marriage, and must comply with the requirements as to solemnisation prescribed by the Marriage Act 1949 as amended. This precludes, for the purpose of contracting a valid marriage, the use of any ceremony not recognised by English law, notwithstanding that one or both of the parties may be foreigners.

59. The law does not simply acknowledge the special status of those who are married: it accords them certain privileges, so that there is a distinction in law between those who are married and those who are cohabiting without marriage. Only in exceptional cases may a married person be compelled to give evidence against a spouse. The children of an unmarried couple are illegitimate and cannot be jointly adopted by their parents. The matrimonial procedures available to a wife to claim financial provision are not available to a cohabitee nor, unlike a wife, has she any right to a property adjustment order when the cohabitation ceases. A man is not entitled to claim an income tax

---

[1]*Nachimson* v. *Nachimson* (1930), p. 217.
[2]*Cheni* v. *Cheni* (1965), P. at p. 89.
[3]*Niboyet* v. *Niboyet* (1878) 4 P.D. at p. 11.

23

allowance for his cohabitee. On the other hand the law now recognises that the cohabiting woman should be protected against violence and molestation from her partner in the same way as a married woman is protected. As a result of the Domestic Violence and Proceedings Act 1976 the cohabitee can obtain an injunction against her partner restraining him from assaulting or molesting her, and in appropriate cases can obtain a court order excluding him from occupation of the house.

Nullity and Divorce

60. English law today provides a general legal procedure whereby validly contracted marriages can be either declared null and void, or terminated; in each case the former partners are left free to remarry. This provision reflects a judgement that it is not in the public interest that the legal semblance of a marriage should be maintained in being when evidence establishes that the substance of the marriage relationship never existed or, having existed, has subsequently broken down.

61. Because marriage is, as we have seen, a legal status arising out of a legal contract, it is necessary to provide a procedure in law for ending a marriage when the circumstances outlined above apply. This is not unique to marriage. A person entering a commercial contract is deemed to intend to fulfil the contract. He may fail to do so for a variety of reasons and the law has to provide for the consequence of that failure, whether it be self-induced or due to some factor beyond his control. The existence of a legal procedure for terminating a contract or status does not in itself affect the nature of the contract or status originally entered upon.

62. The jurisdiction of the courts in nullity cases still largely reflects the older canon law jurisdiction in requiring that any ground on which a decree of nullity is to be based should have been in existence at the time of the marriage ceremony. The civil law and canon law differ at one point, in that at civil law wilful refusal to consummate the marriage makes it possible subsequently to declare the marriage void, though the marriage is not void *ab initio*. This provision, introduced in 1937, has been widely criticised: there is something unsatisfactory in treating an event subsequent to the marriage ceremony as a ground of nullity. However, the Church has hitherto accepted that in law persons whose marriages have been

annulled (whether the marriage was void *ab initio* or voidable) are entitled to be remarried in church, and has acted accordingly.

63.   The divorce jurisdiction of the courts rests on three basic principles. The first, which is entailed by the character of marriage as a status conferred by law, is that that status cannot be terminated solely at the will of the husband or wife. The law requires a judicial sentence in order to alter the relations between the parties and the status of each. To speak of the law as providing for 'divorce by consent' is therefore strictly inaccurate though, as we shall see, in certain circumstances the consent of the couple is an element in obtaining a divorce.

64.   The second principle is that a divorce is granted only when the court is satisfied that the marriage has irretrievably broken down. Breakdown may be proved in one or more of a number of different ways and when so proved the court must grant a decree unless on all the evidence it considers the marriage has not broken down. With the Divorce Reform Act 1969 the law abandoned the concept of the 'matrimonial offence'. It should be said however that for some years prior to the Act that concept was already playing a diminishing role in real decisions.

65.   The third principle on which the present law is—in theory, at least—based is the desirability of achieving a reconciliation between the couple rather than a divorce. The title of the 1969 Act describes it as, *inter alia*, 'An Act . . . to facilitate reconciliation in matrimonial causes . . .'. Though the State and the courts had for some years sanctioned efforts at reconciliation it was not until 1969 that the divorce procedure itself included provisions relating to reconciliation. The solicitor acting for the petitioner is required to certify whether he has drawn to the attention of the parties particulars of persons or agencies qualified to help them. The court is empowered to adjourn proceedings if it appears likely that the possibility of reconciliation exists.

66.   It has to be said that these provisions have proved ineffective in practice through the failure of Parliament to appreciate that by the time spouses have consulted solicitors about a divorce it is generally too late to save the marriage. The recent withdrawal of legal aid from undefended cases has led to a large increase in the number of petitioners conducting their cases in person. Where no solicitor is

engaged no certificate has to be filed in court indicating whether the petitioner has been made aware of particulars of persons or agencies qualified to help effect a reconciliation. In many cases of marriage breakdown the first court application will in fact be to the magistrates' court (where maintenance and custody can be dealt with but not divorce). There is now a very strong case for examining the adequacy of resources available to the magistrates' court for effecting reconciliation, since an application for a maintenance order to this court may be the first public step taken by a couple, and at this stage the breach may not be irreparable.

67.   Reference has already been made to the allegation that the present law provides for, or in effect offers, divorce by consent. The court will grant a decree of divorce if there is firm evidence of two years' separation and of the consent of the respondent spouse. This category of case is sometimes referred to as a 'consent divorce'. It should be emphasised that the decision is the court's, and that it flows from a finding that the marriage has broken down, as evidenced by the fact of separation. We believe it is generally understood that even a consent divorce requires the spouses to submit themselves to the processes of the law. They must have been married for at least three years before a petition can be presented.[1] The court will in the first instance grant a decree nisi; the decree absolute will not be granted unless and until it is satisfied that the arrangements for any children of the marriage are adequate.

68.   The law also provides for a finding of irretrievable breakdown where the parties have been separated for at least five years. If an application for a divorce is made on this ground it is not necessary to secure the consent of the respondent spouse. The court can refuse a divorce when the petition is opposed if it considers that the granting of a decree would result in grave financial or other hardship to the respondent spouse and in all the circumstances it would be wrong to dissolve the marriage. If a decree nisi is granted and the respondent spouse applies to the court for consideration of his or her financial position the decree cannot be made absolute until reasonable financial provision has been made for the respondent, or the petitioner proves that he is unable to provide for the respondent.

---

[1]See Appendix 7, p. 176.

26

69. This provision attracted criticism both when the Divorce Reform Bill was going through Parliament and subsequently, on the ground that for the first time the law was putting spouses in the position where they might be divorced against their will, even though they might be (in common parlance) 'the innocent party'. This criticism reveals ignorance of the way in which the law operated before the 1969 reforms. Ever since 1857, when a civil law on divorce was first introduced, many cases have occurred of people being divorced against their will. The process has been enlarged by the 1969 Act, but the difference is one of degree rather than kind. From 1857 onwards a woman who committed a single act of adultery, but who was otherwise a good wife and mother, could be divorced for that single act. After 1937 a wife who left her husband, but could not prove that he had actually been cruel to her, could be divorced for desertion, even though she did not want a divorce. Likewise a husband who had personality problems and a difficult temperament which adversely affected his wife's health could be guilty of mental cruelty even though he did not intend to be unkind to her. Similarly a person who became mentally ill could be divorced against his wishes after five years, although the mental illness by no means necessarily implied that he did not understand the meaning of divorce, or that he consented to it. The experience of being divorced against one's will was not unknown before the 1969 Act; the significance of that Act in this connexion was in removing a distinction betwen 'guilty' and 'innocent' parties which had hitherto been used to justify such treatment.

70. A variant of the criticism described above has been put to the Commission, namely that as a result of the 1969 Act no-one, whether a Christian or not, who believes that marriage is indissoluble can now enter into marriage in the confidence that he will be able to maintain his commitment to his partner until death ends the bond. Even if one spouse is faithful to the marriage vows, he or she may be unwillingly divorced. In consequence (so it is argued) the intention to form a life-long marriage must in all cases be defective.[1]

71. This eventuality was considered by the Archbishop's Group on the law of divorce. In their report *Putting Asunder* they made the following observations:

> As for those whose unwillingness to have their marriage dissolved stemmed from a conviction that they were committed to their spouses

[1] See in particular the article by Rev. Dr E. Trueman Dicken in *For Better, For Worse* (Church Literature Association, 1977).

irrevocably and for life, they would not be prevented by the action of the Court from maintaining fidelity. The Court would have dissolved the complex of legal rights and duties: it would not . . . have been concerned with any deeper bond. Sometimes, perhaps, the legal freedom to remarry might be a source of temptation to go against conscience: but that is no uncommon experience for a Christian or anyone else whose conscience makes demands not recognised by the society in which he lives. And for those convinced of the real indissolubility of marriage the recommended change in the law would bring at least one advantage: a deserted spouse would no longer be under painful pressure to 'set free' the other party.[1]

72. We share the view thus expressed. We would add that the belief that for a lifelong marriage to be capable of being contracted there must be no possibility of dissolution found no expression in English law before 1969. The law's concern throughout has been with the intentions of the parties as evidenced in their promises to each other at the inception of the marriage. The validity of a marriage in English law is governed by the existence of an intention of the parties at the time to regard it as a life-long monogamous union.

73. Since we began to meet as a Commission public concern has been expressed about the implications of the so-called 'special procedure' system, by which a petitioner puts his evidence in writing in the form of an affidavit instead of attending court to give the same evidence orally in a witness-box. The system was first introduced in December 1975 in undefended cases where no children were involved; it was extended in April 1977 to all undefended cases. In all other respects the procedure of the court is unchanged. In cases where there are children a decree cannot be granted until the court has been satisfied as to the arrangements for them. This is still dealt with by the judge in chambers in all such cases.

74. The object of the changes has been to enable the court to concentrate on the more important matters of custody, applications for financial provision and questions relating to the home. The most recent change was also motivated by a desire to reduce payments out of the Legal Aid Fund at a time of financial stringency. One consequence of the changes has been some loss of formality in divorce proceedings which may not be in the public interest; it should however be borne in mind that even before the special procedure was introduced the majority of hearings lasted less than five minutes each

---

[1] *Op. cit.*, p. 49.

and there was no requirement for the respondent to attend the court. When the special procedure has become better established much of the misunderstanding attaching to it will be dispelled. It is nevertheless unfortunate that it was introduced without prior consultation with the Churches or the legal profession, and without adequate explanation to the public.

75.   In view of the anxieties that have been expressed concerning the significance of the Divorce Reform Act 1969 for the understanding of marriage by our contemporaries, we have considered it necessary to examine the detailed provisions of that Act. Our considered judgement is that the Act has not in any material way altered the law's understanding of what is required of a valid marriage. By introducing the principle of breakdown into the law the 1969 Act may however have given encouragement to a trend which had indeed begun to appear much earlier. That was that the legitimate expectation of emotional and personal growth through marriage would lead to the conclusion that the appropriate and normal response to a failure to achieve emotional satisfaction in marriage was to end the marriage and try again. Our society is increasingly treating divorce as normal and acceptable. While as a Commission we would readily acknowledge that there will be circumstances which on occasion make it necessary that a marriage should be dissolved, we do not think that divorce should be regarded as other than a highly exceptional response to strain and stress within marriage.

CONCLUSION

76.   The changes in the understanding of marriage we have noted equally require a deepening of sensitivity on the part of all, both married couples themselves and also other institutions in society concerned for social health and stability. The task created for the Church, and the courses open to it in discharging that task, are themes to which we turn later in this Report.

77.   In England today marriage, and the continuance of marriage, are matters of free choice, and bear all the stresses and strains which such major decisions involve. The idealisation of love and romance ensures that most couples marry 'for love', though they may over-estimate the part which emotional feelings play in what Christians have always regarded as at least in part a matter of personal will and commitment. Popular songs and women's

magazines do not often stress the fact that emotion is not enough by itself to sustain a loving relationship through time. Marriage needs also to be worked at through mutual adjustment and a degree of self-sacrifice.

78.   Most couples intend to marry 'for life', but the expectation of life is much longer than in earlier generations. A couple marrying in their early twenties will expect to have fifty, if not sixty, years of marriage ahead of them. The amount of time directed to home-making and child-rearing has contracted. The economic independence of the partners both from their parents and from each other is much greater. The kind of life they will lead is less predictable. The social supports available to them are often weaker. At the same time their expectations about the personal and social fulfilment they will find in marriage may be greatly heightened. The couple live out their expectations in a period of violent economic and social fluctuations, where the roles of men and women are less narrowly defined, and where moral and social values appear confused. It is not surprising that so many fail to create stable and lasting marriages. It is surprising, as well as encouraging, that so many succeed.

3
Marriage and Christian Doctrine

'. . . to examine afresh the Christian doctrine of marriage and the marriage discipline of the Church of England . . .'

79.   Marriage holds out the promise and expectation of a new life in a new world. A wedding is an occasion for celebration and joy. The wedding, however, is only the beginning of married life. Because marriage is, humanly speaking, so central and important, it is incumbent on the Church to think clearly and carefully about its character and purpose. Only so will it be able with insight and understanding to prepare those who enter upon marriage in hope and joy. Only so will it be able to meet the needs of those whose experience of marriage turns into failure and defeat. Sound pastoral care must be firmly based on sound doctrine.

80.   Whatever else it may become for those who marry within the fellowship of Christ's religion, marriage is a universal institution which has its origins in nature and society. It does not derive from faith in Jesus Christ and membership of his Church. For this reason we consider that it is more appropriate to speak of 'a Christian doctrine of marriage' than of 'a doctrine of Christian marriage', and we wish to commend our understanding of marriage to our fellow men and women, whether they count themselves Christians or not. In so doing we believe that we are being loyal to the intention of Jesus himself, who in disputing about divorce appealed beyond the law of Moses to God's purposes for marriage 'from the beginning of creation'.[1]

81.   Marriage caters for certain fundamental and universal human needs and potentialities. In the course of history, as we have seen, it has assumed a variety of forms and functions. In spelling out what they believe marriage can be and should be in society today, Christians should gladly acknowledge the insights to be derived from the store of human experience and the findings of the human sciences.

---

[1]Mark 10.6.

82. If, however, they wish to affirm and to commend a particular understanding of marriage, it is because they believe that they have been given a special insight into the deepest needs and potentialities of human nature. This leads them to focus their attention on what a man and a woman can become to each other and through each other, to their own mutual enrichment and to the enrichment of the larger community to which they belong, within a freely covenanted and lifelong relationship of fidelity and love.

83. The primary witness to this special insight is to be found in the Bible, especially in the teaching of Jesus and its interpretation in the writings of the New Testament. A further developing and varied interpretation of this witness is present in the living tradition of the Church. Insight and interpretation interact. They are not given together once and for all. Consequently it is required of Christians, if they wish within this living tradition to be loyal to what has come to them from the past and also responsive to what confronts them in the present, to discriminate as carefully as possible between the substance and its expression, the unchanging and the changing. They may neither accept nor reject without reflection and discernment the movements of social and cultural change, for these are neither necessarily identical with nor necessarily opposed to the providential will of God.

MARRIAGE AND HUMAN EXPERIENCE

84. We have suggested that marriage as a freely covenanted and lifelong relationship of fidelity and love caters for certain fundamental and universal human needs and potentialities. How is this so?

85. It could be argued that it is only a lifelong union between husband and wife which can be expected to provide a secure and stable environment for the nurture of children. Marriage, according to this argument, derives its character from the family. Husband and wife are bound together for the sake of their children, if children there be. As we have seen, this has been until recently the dominant strand in sociological analyses of marriage and the family.

86. Certainly we should not wish to reject this argument altogether. It contains an important element of truth. From biological and social points of view the family is a primary form of human community. Furthermore, from a personal point of view, procreation is a

characteristic expression and fulfilment of married love. The love and care of children are part of the bond uniting husband and wife. Nevertheless, we do not believe that this argument touches the heart of the matter. It suggests that marriage is best understood as 'for' children. We, on the other hand, wish to affirm that marriage is best understood as 'for' husband and wife. It is their relationship with each other which is the basis of marriage. On this is built their relationship with their children. Arguments, therefore, in favour of the life-long nature of the married relationship must be seen to stem from the character of the husband-wife relationship itself, whether or not there are children.

87.   Marriage is a relationship of shared commitment and love. It is a commitment in which nothing is deliberately withheld. As such it is a profound sharing of present experience. As such it also anticipates the sharing of future experience. It is a commitment through time. It embraces the future as well as the present. It intends and promises permanence.

Love

88.   The logic of such intention and promise is as follows. Love in marriage not only unites two persons are they are, it also recreates them as they shall become. It is 'person-making'. If we like, we may call it—even when there are no children—'procreative'. Each partner in the marriage accepts the personal identity of the other, and together they affirm their own personal world. Husband and wife accept responsibility for each other. Indeed the joy of their love is to be found not only in present experience, but also in the acknowledgement of mutual belonging. Such mutual belonging transcends the ebb and flow of experience. 'Many waters cannot quench love, neither can the floods drown it.' It is 'strong as death'. Love in this sense is not only a care and concern for another person in the timelessness of immediate encounter: it is also a continuing and constant care and concern for the other as time flows from the present into the future.

89.   This polyphony of love finds expression in the lovers' bodily union. This is not to be comprehended simply in terms of two individuals' shared experience of ecstatic pleasure. Such it certainly may be; but it is always more. It is an act of personal communication, which spans past, present and future. It is celebration, healing,

renewal, pledge and promise. Sexual intercourse can 'mean' many different things to husband and wife, according to mood and circumstance. Above all it communicates the affirmation of mutual belonging.

90.   Thus the essence of married love is a relationship in which two persons are joined together in a new duality-in-unity and discover a new freedom in interdependence. The fulfilment of the one is inseparable from _ the fulfilment of the other. Such fulfilment encompasses permanence as a goal. If and when the union has had time to take root, no storm of life can tear it up. Or, to change the metaphor, with time a bond is forged between the two which nothing can break asunder.

Commitment to Permanence

91.   Commitment to permanence we see both as an affirmation of the character of the union entered upon and as a means of establishing that union. Marriage is a venture of love in which fulfilment involves vulnerability and hence risk. To love another is to forgo self-sufficiency. It is also to give a hostage to fortune. Human beings are a mixture of strength and frailty. Circumstances beyond their control may militate against a couple's successful marriage. Because of risks like these many today feel that it is lacking in integrity to commit themselves to a love that shall be lifelong. It is not within their power to guarantee the keeping of such a promise. They may honestly hope that it will be lifelong, but they cannot commit themselves.

92.   We understand and respect this unwillingness to be committed to a lifelong relationship. Yet we consider it mistaken. If it is indeed a lifelong relationship which is intended, then it is inadequate simply to hope that it will turn out that way. The deepening and strengthening of the married relationship are not chance occurrences; they depend on the responses that the couple themselves make to occurrences. People *fall* in love; but they do not fall into marriage. Marriage involves the will as well as the emotions. Marriages are *made*. They are 'made' in two senses of the word. They are made initially by mutual consent and commitment. They have still to be made through the sharing of life and love. Some marriages no doubt are easier to make, in this latter sense, than others. If, as a community, we wish them to succeed, then we have a common responsibility to do all in our power to prepare the ground for success. Where the couple themselves are

34

concerned, it is more likely that they will make a success of their marriage if they can take for granted their commitment to each other through fair weather and foul. Such unconditional and lifelong commitment can be an added source of confidence and strength. It can also be a source of freedom and joy, enabling both to be themselves precisely because they know that they belong to each other.

93. We have so far suggested the way in which we should wish to develop our discussion with those who desire marriage to be lifelong, but who hesitate to express a lifelong commitment because of the risks confronting the venture of marriage. There are others, however, who question whether a lifelong relationship is, humanly speaking, for the best. Would it not cater more adequately for human needs if we adopted as our norm a system of 'serial monogamy', by which it became customary for a person to be married two or three times during his lifetime?[1] Human beings have a variety of needs and potentialities which no one person can satisfy. Moreover persons change and develop, and the relationship which satisfies and fulfils at one stage of life may no longer satisfy and fulfil at other stages. The longer the expectation of life, the more, it is argued, there is to be said in favour of serial monogamy.

94. We mention this point of view, not because we think that it is widely held, but because we think that it deserves to be taken seriously. It appeals for support to human nature and human needs, as does our belief in lifelong monogamy. Where, then, lies the difference? In developing an answer to this point of view we should want, while doing justice to the ways in which persons change in the course of a lifetime, to do equal justice to the aspect of personal continuity. To become a person is indeed to be capable of change; but if change is to be growth, then in and through the change there must also be a pattern of constancy and reliability. We believe that a lifelong relationship of fidelity and love can provide the best environment in which two persons can discover themselves in and through each other. The exclusiveness of the marriage relationship is justified, not because it can claim to satisfy all the needs and potentialities of the couple—marriage should not be expected to provide the sole, sufficient human community—but because it

---

[1]The concept of 'serial monogamy' was discussed in Robert Chester, 'Family and Marriage in the Post-Parental Years', in *Marriage Guidance*, Vol. 14, No. 11 (September 1973).

provides the basis for a union between two persons in which there is total and ungrudging acceptance and commitment within a shared world. This is an element in married love which is far more fundamental than the satisfaction of any particular physical or psychological need. It envisages a growth and fulfilment in relationship to be achieved by way of self-forgetfulness as much as self-affirmation, by self-giving as much as self-seeking. The exclusiveness of this relationship includes, we believe, sexual exclusiveness. It is sometimes argued that extra-marital sexual relationships are not incompatible with marital fidelity, and that they can even enrich a marriage. Almost always, however, extra-marital sexual relationships are likely to threaten, if not to destroy, a marriage. Furthermore, if sexual intercourse is taken, as we have suggested (see para. 89), to signify an unspoken affirmation of mutual belonging, then extra-marital sex 'says' something which is not the case. It makes of the married sexual relationship a deception and a lie.

The Marriage Bond
95. We are concerned not only with the possibility and the desirability of a lifelong relationship of married love, but also with the character of the relationship itself. We have spoken of forging a bond which nothing can break asunder. This bond is made up of many different strands. It is a moral bond, deriving from a promise of fidelity. It is an emotional bond, deriving from shared experiences. It is a physical bond, deriving from sexual union. It is a spiritual bond deriving from allegiance to common values. It is a bond of habit: 'I've grown accustomed to her face'. It is above all a personal bond, weaving together some or all of these various strands. What gives to this personal bond its point and purpose is mutual love. It is this love which is 'the bond of perfectness'.

96. The marriage bond unites two flesh-blood-and-spirit persons. It makes them the persons that they are. It binds them together, not in any casual or peripheral fashion, but at the very centre of their being. They become the persons they are through their relationship to each other. Each might say to the other: 'I am I and I am you; together you and I are we'. Since the marriage bond is in this way a bond of personal *being*, it is appropriate to speak of it as having an 'ontological' character.

97. All of us are agreed that, in its perfectness, the marriage bond unites two persons at the centre of their being, that it is in this sense an ontological bond. All of us are agreed that there actually occur such ontological unions between man and wife, unions which, as a matter of fact, nothing can dissolve. We are not all agreed, however, how we are to describe those unions which, to all outward appearances, have broken down.

98. The view was expressed and defended among us that, even when a marriage had broken down and reconciliation was, at least humanly speaking, no longer possible, some bond between husband and wife still existed. This bond followed upon their free and responsible commitment to each other until parted by death. Whether their marriage was a 'success' or not, the commitment had been made and the bond established. The fullness of the marriage relationship was indeed made up of many and varied ingredients. It needed constantly to be deepened and renewed in life and love. The marriage bond, however, did not depend on the continued flowering of the relationship, but was, rather, that which founded the relationship. It was an 'ontological' bond in a further sense of the word, in as much as it was impervious to time and change, participating in the eternity of being. The bond, once made, could not be unmade. Even if husband and wife separated—as sometimes also parents and children, or brothers and sisters, separate—and entered into new alliances, the original bond would remain—as does the bond between those who share a common ancestry. Whatever the state might do in granting a legal divorce, and whatever the pastor might counsel the husband and wife who had separated from each other and were thinking of forming new alliances, the fact of their having entered into a lifelong commitment in marriage remained of continuing significance and validity. It might be ignored or disavowed: it could never be expunged. Hence, whatever might be said and done, a second marriage, while the partner in the original marriage still lived, was a kind of contradiction in terms. An ontological bond still existed.

99. Most of us, however, while sympathetic to the underlying concern and general thrust of this argument, were unable to accept its conclusion. We too wished to stress the importance of a lifelong commitment. Such a commitment established the beginning and looked forward to the fulfilment of marriage. It set up a binding covenant, within the context of which the marriage relationship

might be free to develop. Nevertheless, the bond which was established by consent and commitment was not to be identified outright with the ontological bond which united two persons at the centre of their being and which, in its perfectness, was in fact unbreakable. This latter bond was not simply a bond of commitment grounded in promise and obligation. It was a relational bond of personal love, a compound of commitment, experience and response, in which the commitment clothed itself in the flesh and blood of a living union. The commitment looked forward to this deeper union of love. Indeed, in faith it anticipated and proclaimed it. Nevertheless, *this deeper union had still to be realised.* Without such a union the commitment itself did not achieve its proper end. For the commitment was not merely that each should 'keep only unto' the other, but that each should also 'love, comfort and honour' the other until parted by death. The commitment was made in love and for love. In one sense, the commitment made, the marriage already existed. But in another sense, the making of the marriage was a continuing process. The bond of commitment had to realise itself as a bond of love. Where love and cherishing had ceased, the marriage was breaking down. Where there was no possibility of rekindling this love, the breakdown was irretrievable. A living relationship had finally died. It is true that what had been could never be made as if it had not been. In this sense the slate could not be wiped clean. Nevertheless, the covenant had been broken beyond repair. No ontological bond now existed. It was for the individuals to decide what each of them must do in face of the fact that the 'vow and covenant betwixt them made' had come to nothing. It was for the courts to decide what action to take over the legal bond, if one or both the partners concluded that the marriage had ended.

100. In short, we are all agreed in affirming that indissolubility is characteristic of marriage as it should and can be. There is something radically wrong when a marriage does break down. Marriages *ought* to be indissoluble! However, most of us reject the doctrine that marriages *cannot* by definition be dissolved. It is only too possible for men and women in particular cases to break the bond which God, in principle and in general, wills to be unbreakable, and to put asunder what God, in his original purpose, has joined together. Therein lies the measure of human failure and sin.

101. Our discussion of the marriage bond reflects not only our

desire to clarify our understanding of marriage but also our practical pastoral concern. We need to ask how men and women who enter upon marriage can be helped to realise that deeper union to which their original commitment looks forward in promise and hope. Furthermore, where promise and hope have been frustrated and a marriage has in fact irretrievably broken down, we need to consider how the evil done can best be contained and future good promoted. What practical response is likely to meet the needs of individual men and women, while at the same time doing justice to our fundamental perception of what marriage can and should be?

THE TESTIMONY OF THE BIBLE

102. Thus far we have been reflecting on the nature of marriage in the light of human experience and insight. It might be said that we had been putting forward a natural theology of marriage. We turn now to revelation and its primary witness in the Bible. Here too we have to discriminate between the changing and the unchanging, the substance and its expression. The witness of the New Testament comes to us from a specific cultural context, and we are constrained to keep in mind the distinction between that which is of permanent and that which is of only transient value and significance.

103. It is fitting that we should ask first, as of primary importance, what Jesus himself taught about marriage. Any considered answer to this question has to take into account both the meagreness and the character of the gospel evidence. On the one hand, the recorded words of Jesus concerning marriage occur, for the most part, in contexts in which he is speaking of divorce rather than of marriage. On the other hand, they show signs of having been expanded and adapted to answer practical questions which had arisen in the life of the early Church, where differing Jewish and Gentile cultural customs obtained. The recorded words afford us access to the mind of Christ, but the mind of Christ cannot be simply and immediately read off the recorded words.

The Words of Jesus

104. The immediately relevant gospel sayings enshrine two basic statements. These are (a) a statement by Jesus about marriage, given in reply to a question concerning the legitimacy of divorce (Mark 10.

2-9, cf. Matthew 19. 3-8); and (b) a saying of Jesus about divorce, remarriage and adultery (given in varying forms in Mark 10. 11-12; Matthew 5. 31-32; Matthew 19. 9; and Luke 16. 18). Further indirect evidence of Jesus' teaching can be gained from Matthew 5. 27-28, when he equates the lustful look with the act of adultery; from Matthew 19. 10-12, when he speaks of those who have made themselves eunuchs for the sake of the kingdom of heaven; and Mark 12. 18-27, with parallels in Matthew 22. 23-33 and Luke 20. 27-40, when he affirms that in the resurrection of the dead there is neither marrying nor giving in marriage.

105. For convenience we include some of the material which incorporates the substance of Jesus' two basic statements:

> And Pharisees came up and in order to test him asked, 'Is it lawful for a man to divorce his wife?' He answered them, 'What did Moses command you?' They said, 'Moses allowed a man to write a certificate of divorce, and to put her away.' But Jesus said to them, 'For your hardness of heart he wrote you this commandment. But from the beginning of creation, "God made them male and female." "For this reason a man shall leave his father and mother and be joined to his wife, and the two shall become one." So they are no longer two but one. What therefore God has joined together, let no man put asunder.' (Mark 10. 2-9)

> 'Whoever divorces his wife and marries another, commits adultery against her; and if she divorces her husband and marries another, she commits adultery.' (Mark 10. 11-12)

> 'Whoever divorces his wife, except for unchastity, and marries another, commits adultery.' (Matthew 19. 9)

> 'Every one who divorces his wife and marries another commits adultery, and he who marries a woman divorced from her husband commits adultery.' (Luke 16. 18)[1]

106. In answering the question concerning the legitimacy of divorce Jesus is recorded in both and Markan and the Matthaean versions as asserting the permanence of marriage. He appeals to Genesis to confirm the unity of husband and wife, for here is expressed the will of God; and he forbids men to put asunder what God has joined together. Moses had indeed allowed divorce in certain circumstances, but this was a concession to human weakness.

107. In recording Jesus' saying about divorce, remarriage and adultery—a saying which varies in form from gospel to gospel, probably reflecting the detailed differences of Jewish and Roman divorce practices—Matthew differs significantly from Mark and

[1]RSV.

Luke. They all agree in having Jesus assert that divorce and remarriage involve adultery, but in Matthew's version Jesus makes an exception of 'unchastity'. The precise meaning of the Greek word *porneia* is disputed. The traditional translation is 'adultery', but it may have a broader connotation.

108. According to Jewish law divorce of his wife by a husband was permitted, but there was disagreement concerning the grounds on which such divorce might be permitted. Matthew has Jesus express a strict interpretation of the meaning and extent of the Mosaic concession, whereas Mark has him over-ride the Mosaic concession altogether by appealing to the original will of God. We take the view that Mark is here closer than Matthew to the actual thought of Jesus. It seems likely that Matthew presents us with an adaptation of Jesus' saying in which his original words have been interpreted and applied to certain practical problems of marriage breakdown in a Jewish-Christian community. Further support of this view may be found in the consideration that Jesus' teaching concerning divorce was unlikely to have created the stir that it obviously did (*cf.* Matthew 19. 10), had it not appeared to involve a rejection of the Mosaic concession rather than an interpretation of it, an interpretation which, however strict, was nevertheless widely held.

109. We note in passing that a critical scholarly approach to the gospels, such as underlies the judgement expressed in the preceding paragraph, results in an affirmation that Jesus' original saying about divorce, remarriage and adultery allowed for no exceptions. A more traditional approach, on the other hand, which takes Jesus' recorded sayings at their face value, and gives to the Matthaean account an authority and weight equal to that which it gives to the Markan account, results in the admission that Jesus did not always condemn divorce and remarriage but made an exception in cases of *porneia*.

110. At this stage of our reflections this much is clear: Jesus taught that marriage, according to God's will in creation, was lifelong, and that husband and wife were 'one'. What is not so clear is, first, the precise significance which this teaching has within the total context of Jesus' proclamation of the kingdom of God and his own ministry of challenge, forgiveness and renewal; and, second, how the Church is to be faithful to the mind of Christ in developing a doctrine of marriage and a sound pastoral care for all those married people it comes into contact with, not least those whose marriages have broken down.

111. We may hope to shed further light on these difficult and delicate matters if we ask ourselves two related questions concerning Jesus and law. What was Jesus' attitude to the Law of Moses? Did he intend his teaching to be a new Law for his own disciples?

112. These questions do not permit of straightforward and assured answers. The evidence is at best circumstantial and indirect. Nevertheless the following considerations are to the point.

113. There are good grounds for believing that the religious authorities of his time opposed Jesus in the conviction that he was setting his own authority above that of the Law of Moses. Since the Law of Moses was believed to be of divine origin, Jesus would thus be exalting the authority of a man above that of God.

114. Could the authorities have established the truth of their conviction beyond all possible doubt, they would have had unexceptionable grounds for condemning Jesus publicly and unequivocally. On more than one occasion they appear to have attempted to trap Jesus into incriminating himself on this very point; but Jesus did not let himself be trapped in this way. Even over the question concerning divorce, which may well have been intended as just such a trap, Jesus' answer did not give the authorities the evidence that they needed, for his condemnation of divorce was couched in an appeal from the Law, as written in Deuteronomy, to the Law, as written in Genesis.

115. From the fact that the authorities tried to trap him it is clear that Jesus' teaching must have been understood to run counter to the Law of Moses, and in that respect to have legislative implications. It is possible to argue that he was simply abrogating the authority of the Law, but that the religious authorities were never able to secure foolproof and indisputable evidence of this fact. To most of us, however, a reading and assessment of the gospel evidence suggests otherwise. Jesus was certainly a radical critic of the contemporary interpretation and application of the Law. Instead of its being instruction in the way of life it had been made into an unbearable burden. The demands of legalism had been substituted for the challenge of grace. Jesus refused to discuss detailed issues of right and wrong in these terms; he pointed men back to the source and resource of life and love.

116. So it was with regard to the right and wrong of this and that ground for divorce. Religious debate about the extent of a husband's rights in divorcing his wife misunderstood the whole thrust of the law of life. Marriage was for life—in every sense of that word. Husband and wife were no longer two separate individuals, adjusting their relationship in terms of a nicely calculated less or more. They were interdependent. The life of each was the life of the other. Divorce and remarriage shattered this unity-in-duality as completely as adultery.

117. Jesus rejected all talk of claim and counter-claim. He saw things in a totally different light. His words, therefore, were often paradoxical and disturbing. We may hazard the suggestion that, in replying to a question about the legitimacy of divorce, Jesus cut through the whole tangle of debate about legitimacy with some such saying as 'He who divorces his wife commits adultery', and that his more prosaic and practically-minded followers tried to turn this biting aphorism into solid case-law by introducing the idea of remarriage and adapting the saying to the cultural conditions of their various environments.

118. If our interpretation of the main thrust and tenor of Jesus' teaching is correct, it follows that he was not establishing new legislation to supersede the Law of Moses. Nor was he directly concerned with matters of pastoral discipline. Rather, he was calling his hearers to get their basic idea of marriage straight. He intended his words to be taken with the utmost seriousness. Marriage is for life. Husband and wife form a new kind of unity. Divorce is as destructive of this unity as adultery.

119. It would be inadequate to speak of Jesus' teaching as setting forth no more than an ideal. It is insight, instruction and admonition. It establishes the character and moral norm of marriage. From this point of view divorce is as unthinkable as adultery. So, too, is the whole idea of marriage breakdown. Nevertheless, the unthinkable can happen. Marriages can and do break down. The Church has to proceed from doctrine to discipline. In Matthew we see, perhaps, how one Christian community took this step. *Porneia*, it was felt, broke the marriage bond beyond repair. In this instance divorce—and presumably in many cases remarriage—was to be permitted. The damage done, this way of repairing a broken situation was consistent with the mind of Christ.

120.   From Jesus' other sayings to which we have drawn attention (see para. 104) we can venture the following inferences and suggestions. His equation of the lustful glance with adultery is a similar kind of aphorism to his equation of divorce with adultery. Both sayings are paradoxical. Neither can be construed as legislation. Both are to be taken with the utmost seriousness as expressing insight and challenge. Jesus' sayings about the vocation to celibacy in this life for the sake of God's kingdom and the absence of marriage in the resurrection life may have the same significance. In the fullness of God's purposes all our relationships will be characterised by that depth of love which now we can know only in marriage. Marriage offers in this life the deepest union of one human being with another. But depth is achieved at the price of exclusiveness. Marriage, therefore, is no substitute for life in God's kingdom. The celibate uses his sexuality in this life to bear witness to the universality of love, although his relationships with others lack the totality of body and spirit which belongs to husband and wife. Both the married and the celibate together witness to the richness of the community of love to which God calls men in Jesus Christ.

121.   We conclude our discussion of Jesus' teaching by reiterating that there is little doubt about the essential content of Jesus' two sayings on marriage and divorce. Where interpretation of their full significance begins—and with interpretation room for disagreement —we have wished to attribute to them the utmost importance for our understanding of what marriage is all about. Nevertheless, we have refused to see in them either legislation or direct pastoral instruction, although some of us believe that they must have some legislative import and hence a bearing on matters of pastoral discipline. Nor do these sayings decisively settle the question whether Jesus thought that marriage was indissoluble, although most of us are of the opinion that he cast no doubt on the *reality* of divorce and remarriage according to the Mosaic concession and in fact assumed that man could break the bond which God willed to be permanent.

From Doctrine to Discipline
122.   The movement from doctrine to discipline, which we have already seen at work in Matthew (para. 119 above), we can observe again in the writings of Paul, especially in I Corinthians 7, part of which for convenience we quote:

The husband should give to his wife her conjugal rights, and likewise the wife to her husband. For the wife does not rule over her own body, but the husband does; likewise the husband does not rule over his own body, but the wife does. (vv. 3-4)
To the unmarried and the widows I say that it is well for them to remain single as I do. (v. 8)
To the married I give charge, not I but the Lord, that the wife should not separate from her husband (but if she does, let her remain single or else be reconciled to her husband)—and that the husband should not divorce his wife. To the rest I say, not the Lord, that if any brother has a wife who is an unbeliever, and she consents to live with him, he should not divorce her. If any woman has a husband who is an unbeliever, and he consents to live with her, she should not divorce him. For the unbelieving husband is consecrated through his wife, and the unbelieving wife is consecrated through her husband. Otherwise, your children would be unclean, but as it is they are holy. But if the unbelieving partner desires to separate, let it be so; in such a case the brother or sister is not bound. For God has called us to peace. Wife, how do you know whether you will save your husband? Husband, how do you know whether you will save your wife? (vv. 10-16)[1]

123.   Paul is here dealing with actual pastoral problems: he is formulating practical rules. He follows the lines laid down by Jesus. His recommendation of celibacy is in accord with Jesus' own practice, as well as with his sayings about the celibate's vocation and the resurrection life. His charge not to divorce is derived explicitly from 'the Lord', thus ascribing to Jesus' utterance the authority of law. No Christian is to divorce his marriage partner. But what is to happen if a believer—perhaps a convert—is married to an unbeliever? What if, as the passage seems to suggest, the unbeliever proposes to end the marriage if the believer does not abandon his or her Christian faith? Paul has to apply Jesus' teaching to a case which it does not obviously fit. Carefully distinguishing his own judgement from that of 'the Lord', he affirms that the marriage must be allowed to come to an end. It is of less importance than perseverance in the faith. The believer is no longer 'bound'. Whether the believer is free to marry again in these circumstances is disputable, but there is no explicit indication that this is not the case. Tradition has, on the whole, taken it to be the case.

124.   In both Matthew and Paul we discern the movement from doctrine to discipline; from principle to practice; from insight and challenge to institution and law. The movement occurs because of the determination to be loyal to the mind of Christ, in both his stringency

[1]RSV.

45

and his compassion, and at the same time to minister to the needs of men and women in their actual situations.

A Sacramental Union

125. We turn finally to consider a passage in the Epistle to the Ephesians:

> Be subject to one another out of reverence for Christ. Wives, be subject to your husbands, as to the Lord. For the husband is the head of the wife as Christ is the head of the church, his body, and is himself its Saviour. As the church is subject to Christ, so let wives be subject in everything to their husbands. Husbands, love your wives, as Christ loved the church and gave himself up for her, that he might sanctify her, having cleansed her by the washing of water with the word, that the church might be presented before him in splendour, without spot or wrinkle or any such thing, that she might be holy and without blemish. Even so husbands should love their wives as their own bodies. He who loves his wife loves himself. For no man ever hates his own flesh, but nourishes and cherishes it as Christ does the church, because we are members of his body. 'For this reason a man shall leave his father and mother and be joined to his wife, and the two shall become one.' This is a great mystery, and I take it to mean Christ and the church; however, let each one of you love his wife as himself, and let the wife see that she respects her husband. (5. 21-33)[1]

126. This passage introduced a new dimension into the Christian reflection on marriage and has proved a source of inspiration for many Christian couples through the ages. At its heart is an analogy between the relationship between husband and wife and the relationship between Christ and his Church. Marriage is 'an honourable estate, instituted of God in the time of man's innocency, signifying unto us the mystical union that is betwixt Christ and his Church' (Book of Common Prayer).

127. In expounding this analogy—for that is what it is—we do well to remember that we are dealing only with descriptive comparisons, not with exact equivalences or dogmatic definitions. Thus, for example, the relation between Christ and the Church is here compared with that between head and body. However, other images and comparisons are used elsewhere in the New Testament. Christ can be described as the first-born among many brothers: so the faithful become his younger brothers in the family of God the Father. In interpreting analogies we must use insight and judgement. It would be a mistake to press an analogy uncritically at every point. In

[1]RSV.

this instance the important thing is to set side by side the unity between husband and wife and the unity between Christ and his Church, to allow them to illuminate each other and to reflect in this light on the nature of married love and the marriage bond.

128. The passage occurs in a part of the epistle in which the writer gives advice to Gentile Christians on the manner of life appropriate to those who have 'learnt Christ'. For each and every status—whether that of a wife, a husband, a child, or even of a slave—there is a way of life which demonstrates what it means to live 'in the Lord'. Although specific demands will vary, this 'way' can be summed up in the injunction to 'be subject to one another out of reverence for Christ', that is, to be people discerning Christ in and through each other. The slave, for example, is to obey his master single-mindedly, 'as serving Christ': he is in effect to be Christ's slave. Masters must give up using threats: both master and man have the same Master in heaven.

129. Similarly, wives and husbands are to express in their mutual relationship a love and care which are a response to Christ's love for each of them. The natural relationship of a wife to her husband is, for the writer, one of subordination, and it is this which gives the analogy its immediate application. In urging wives, however, to be subject to their husbands 'as to the Lord' the writer, while assuming the givenness and propriety of such subordination, nevertheless envisages a transformation in the way in which it is to be expressed. In like manner the husband's exercise of authority over his wife is to be transformed in response to the mysterious working of God's love. Without ceasing to be authoritative it is to be characterised by the self-giving devotion which marks Christ's love for his church.

130. The writer, as we have said, accepted without question the authority of husbands over wives, just as he accepted without question the right of masters to own slaves. Both ideas were part and parcel of the prevailing culture of the day. Christians of other cultures, however, are not bound by their regard for Scripture to accept either. Some indeed would claim, as would most of us, that the historical processes, noted in the last chapter, by which ideas of authority and subordination in marriage have been largely superseded by expectations of sharing and equality, reflect the movement of the Holy Spirit no less than did the abolition of slavery. They can see nothing in nature or in revelation which gives to husbands an unalterable and indisputable right to the obedience of their wives. Any fixed hierarchy

of order or separation of roles is to be questioned in the name of human dignity and Christian liberty. It is for each partner to marriage to offer to the other the best of which he or she is capable, and for both together to work out an appropriate pattern for their married life.

131. Disagreement over the issues of authority and subordination in marriage need not, however, prevent us from accepting and appreciating the writer's central point. He is concerned more with the quality of the marriage relationship than with its structure. This quality will be transformed by the reciprocal love and respect which flow from the fact of its being 'in the Lord'. Marriage, as envisaged in this epistle, is a union which issues from love and continues in love, no matter how in any instance it may be patterned and expressed.

132. As a corollary the passage suggests another important insight. Married love—and let us not forget that this includes sexual love—is not to be set over against and contrasted with divine love. Were such a contrast valid, the basis for the whole analogy would be lacking. Marriage is an order of natural love which reflects, and at its deepest participates in, the order of divine love. God's love is creative, self-giving and utterly faithful. Married love can be the same. It is open to grace. Our sexual and erotic natures may be seen as a providential opportunity given to us by God for learning more and more of the life of love in all its heights and depths. Marriage will be purified and deepened when it is undertaken 'in Christ'. The love of husband and wife for each other will at the same time be a love for God in and through each other and a love for each other in God.

133. To develop the analogy in this way is to develop, in the wider but important sense of the word, a 'sacramental' theology of marriage, which does justice both to the rooting of marriage in nature and society and to its purification and completion in the redemptive love of God. Human love becomes the medium of divine love, in which it also participates. Thus the vocation of those who marry 'in Christ' is to show in their life together, in their unity-in-duality, what love between a man and a woman, within the enabling, forgiving and renewing context of God's creative and redemptive love, can and shall become.

134. To develop the analogy still further, as has sometimes happened, and to affirm on this basis that marriage between the

baptised is a sacrament of the Church, instituted by Christ, and that in this sacrament husband and wife are joined together by God in a union which no power on earth can dissolve, is, we believe, mistaken. It is not hard to understand how such a development has occurred. Nevertheless, we are unanimous in our conviction that it strains the witness of Scripture beyond what it can reasonably support.

135. It is true that the writer of the epistle, by referring to Christ's act of sacrificial love on the cross, has introduced by analogy the idea of a redemptive element into the understanding of marriage too. Nevertheless, marriage still belongs properly to the order of creation, and to erect it into a sacrament of the Church is to risk confounding the order of creation with the order of redemption and to suggest too sharp a distinction between 'natural' marriage and 'Christian' marriage. Furthermore, it is to press the analogy in the text to a use beyond that which it can bear. For the comparison is not between Christ's once and for all work of redemption on the cross and the once and for all commitment of a man and a woman to each other, but between Christ's continuing love, displayed on the cross and nourishing the Church, and the continuing love which husbands are exhorted to show their wives. It is the relationship between husband and wife rather than the act of commitment which the analogy illuminates.

136. The fact that the Latin word used in the Vulgate to translate the Greek word *mysterion* is *sacramentum* provides no support for the view that marriage is one of the 'sacraments' of the Church. We may quote from the classic commentary on *Ephesians* by J. Armitage Robinson: 'The Latin rendering *sacramentum hoc magnum est* well represents the Greek: for "sacramentum" combines the ideas of the symbol and its meaning. It is hardly necessary to point out that it does not imply that St. Paul is here speaking of marriage as a sacrament in the later sense'.

137. We do not accept the view that marriage between baptised Christians is a sacrament and *as such* indissoluble. Nevertheless the question still remains whether marriage is indissoluble simply because it is marriage. What does the analogy suggest on this point?

138. Granted that there is no explicit assertion that marriages cannot be dissolved, an argument for their indissolubility can be developed from the analogy, if not by way of logical deduction, at least

by way of logical congruity. It is inconceivable that Christ should cease to love the Church. Therefore the union between Christ and the Church is indissoluble; and this union extends to weak and sinful men. (Whether it also extends to those who have been baptised, but who have afterwards rejected Christ, is known, perhaps, only to God himself. The analogy, as we have said before, is not to be pressed beyond reason.) It can therefore be argued that, just as it is inconceivable that the union between Christ and his Church should be dissolved, so it is inconceivable that the union between husband and wife should be dissolved. In this way marriage resembles baptism. Once baptised, always baptised: baptism can never be repeated.

139.   We recognise the appeal of this argument for indissolubility. We agree that the analogy affords a strong exhortation that marriages should not be dissolved. As we have already said in another context (para. 100), there is something radically wrong when a marriage does break down. And this is especially true of a marriage 'in Christ'. Nevertheless, most of us reject the doctrine that marriages, especially marriages 'in Christ', *cannot* ultimately be dissolved and do not consider that it derives cogency from the analogy with the union between Christ and his Church. Irretrievable breakdown *can* disrupt the bond, even more surely and tragically than death. When, therefore, we have said all that ought to be said about the resources for reconciliation and the means of grace which are available to believers, even so we have to recognise the actualities of failure and sin among believers as well as among unbelievers. What we may hope for, call for and even perhaps expect from believers is not always what comes to pass. In the end fidelity in love is of grace, not of law. The resources of divine love are infinite, but they are not irresistible.

140.   We do not wish to end this section on a negative note. The deep, 'ontological' union in love between man, wife and God is a treasure which cannot be too highly valued. It is, in its way, a foretaste of God's kingdom. Its fashioning involves sacrifice as well as fulfilment, pain as well as delight. But its attainment is joy, a joy which is to be found not only 'at the end of the journey', but also in the journeying. We believe that Christians have a 'high' doctrine of marriage which they are called to commend in word and deed to the world.

141. The story of the developing and varied interpretation of the biblical witness concerning marriage and divorce in the living tradition of the Church is not for us to repeat. It has already been told by authorities such as E. Schillebeeckx in *Marriage: Secular Reality and Saving Mystery* (Sheed and Ward 1965) and A. R. Winnett in his two books, *Divorce and Remarriage in Anglicanism* (Macmillan 1958) and *The Church and Divorce, A Factual Survey* (Mowbray 1968). We shall content ourselves with a number of general observations and comments.

142. The Church has always upheld life-long monogamy as the characteristic moral norm of marriage. On the other hand it has not always justified this norm in terms of the relationship between husband and wife. Where justification other than the authority of the teaching of Jesus has been sought, it has too often been found only in the procreation of children or sometimes even in the provision of a remedy against fornication. For centuries marriage has been widely rated as a second best to virginity, and sexual intercourse has been virtually equated with lust. The idea of a covenant of love between husband and wife, expressed in bodily as well as spiritual union, has had a hard struggle to find favour and commendation. It is arguable that the acceptance of this idea has owed as much to insight gained from the human sciences as to doctrine developed in ecclesiastical tradition.

143. The Church has always recognised the necessity in certain cases of a separation between husband and wife, even though such separation clearly contravenes the norm of life-long union in love. For example adultery, and other offences which may be classified as adultery, have been considered justifiable grounds for releasing one partner to a marriage from living with the other partner. Christians, however, it has been taught, should always wait and hope for forgiveness, reconciliation and renewal of the marriage.

144. 'Christians should . . .' Such was the broad principle. Divorce and remarriage were something which ought not to be. For Christians they were 'unthinkable'. Nevertheless, there is clear evidence that in both the Eastern and the Western Church during the first millennium divorce and remarriage were sometimes allowed. In certain cases they might be for the best.

145. 'Is the broad principle to be regarded as a law binding universally and unconditionally? If any exceptions are to be allowed, in what cases do they apply? Should man and woman stand on the same footing as regards the right to claim divorce? Should any difference be made between cases where both partners are professing Christians and those in which one is an unbeliever or a heretic? These and similar questions have from century to century occupied the attention of Christian teachers and legislators.'[1]

146. The Orthodox Churches have by and large continued the tradition of teaching and practice developed in the first millennium. Marriage is characteristically for time and eternity. The union between husband and wife is so close that death itself does not dissolve it. A second marriage, after the death of one of the partners, is to be avoided. It is not, however, impossible; and in certain circumstances it may be the best course to advise. God's relation to his family is not, primarily, that of a lawgiver, issuing laws which 'never shall be broken', but that of a father, seeking to bring out of each situation that which is best for members of his household. What is in this way 'best' may differ from what is, ideally and absolutely, good. Furthermore, a marriage may break down during the lifetime of both partners. Separation may be necessary. In certain circumstances it may be for the best that separation should be formalised in divorce and that a second marriage should be entered upon. Such action too, although out of accord with God's original will and intention for marriages in general, may in these circumstances accord with his will for these two persons in particular. He is a God of both order and compassion.

147. It has sometimes been suggested that the Orthodox Churches have in their discipline and practice been too accommodating to the social standards of their surrounding cultures. Against this it may be argued that these Churches have been nearer to the mind of Christ, and have better maintained the balance between his demand and his compassion, than other Churches which have gone to one extreme or another.

148. In the medieval period the Church in the West developed its doctrine of marriage in a new direction and accordingly modified its practice. 'In the scholastic view of marriage which was elaborated in

[1]James Hastings, *Encyclopaedia of Religion and Ethics,*. Vol. VIII, p. 438.

the twelfth and thirteenth centuries the *sacramentum* was not seen purely as a symbol, but as an effective symbol which brought something about—an objective bond that could not be broken. According to the church Fathers the dissolution of marriage was not *permissible;* but according to the schoolmen its dissolution was not *possible.'*[1] Schillebeeckx goes on to affirm that this development in doctrine did no more than draw out the full meaning of the biblical witness: 'These two visions—the patristic view of marriage as a moral obligation and the scholastic view of marriage as an ontological bond—are not mutually exclusive, but rather mutually implicit. Both the patristic and the scholastic doctrines are firmly based on scripture'.[2]

149.   Most of us find ourselves unable to accept Schillebeeckx's assertions without qualification. We can all agree that the patristic and the scholastic 'visions' were mutually implicit. Both 'saw' marriage as life-long commitment and unbreakable union. But when it is a matter of the articulation of this 'vision' in terms of 'ontological' bonds, we find that basically the same difference of opinion rises among us here as when we were discussing the natural theology of marriage (see paras. 98 and 99). Most of us wish to distinguish between two different uses of the word 'ontological'. If we take it to mean 'penetrating to the centre of personal being', then we accept the judgement that the moral and the ontological interpretations of the marriage bond are mutually implicit, and that they are both consonant with Scripture. If, on the other hand, we take 'ontological' to mean 'eternal and absolutely indissoluble', then we cannot all accept the judgement that the two interpretations are mutually implicit; nor can we all agree that Scripture demands an ontological interpretation of the marriage bond. We can understand how such a view may be developed from one possible interpretation of the analogy in Ephesians 5 (*cf.* para. 138). When, however, we have taken all the biblical evidence into account, most of us find it impossible to accept the suggestion that it sets forward a doctrine of absolute indissolubility.

150.   Having developed the doctrine of the indissoluble bond, and so having committed itself to the view that divorce from this bond was something which no power on earth could effect, the Church in the

---

[1]Schillebeeckx, *op. cit.*, II, p. 70.
[2]*Ibid.*

West still had to deal pastorally with weak and sinful men and women. The only way which its newly developed doctrine made possible was by enlarging the grounds of nullity. If it could be established that what had appeared to be a valid marriage contract was not in fact a valid contract, then the 'marriage' was no marriage at all, and those who had contracted marriage invalidly were now free to marry for the first time. The number of relationships which were treated as falling within the prohibited degrees of marriage steadily increased, comprehending not only remote blood-ties but also 'spiritual' relationships such as that between a god-parent and a god-child. In the small self-contained communities in which most people lived it was hard to be certain that one was not marrying within the prohibited degrees.

151. By the eve of the Reformation the traffic in annulments thus made possible had reached such scandalous proportions that it was claimed that no marriage was safe and that the institution of marriage was itself threatened. The Reformers, appealing from canon law to the Bible, radically reduced the number of impediments to marriage which they were prepared to countenance. At the same time, judging that the institution of marriage would not be strengthened by an absolute prohibition of divorce, and following their interpretation of Jesus' teaching as recorded in Matthew, they permitted divorce in the case of adultery and of desertion—which was counted as an equivalent sin—and, with divorce, the right to remarry. In taking this step they rejected the scholastic doctrine of an indissoluble metaphysical bond. Luther established the life-long union between husband and wife on the basis of a solemn contract before God and the sacredness of the promises so made. Calvin continued to speak of a bond (*vinculum*); but it was a bond which *God* had forged, and what God had forged God himself could dissolve, which in the case of adultery was exactly what God did.

ANGLICAN DOCTRINE SINCE THE REFORMATION

152. The Church of England, Catholic and Reformed, has never officially committed itself to the scholastic doctrine of the indissolubility of the marriage bond. Nor, on the other hand, has it officially repudiated it and committed itself to a Lutheran or a Calvinist doctrine. Its most recent authoritative statement is to be found in the revised Canon B 30 (1969):

The Church of England affirms, according to our Lord's teaching, that marriage is in its nature a union permanent and life-long, for better for worse, till death them do part, of one man with one woman, to the exclusion of all others on either side, for the procreation and nurture of children, for the hallowing and right direction of the natural instincts and affections, and for the mutual society, help, and comfort which the one ought to have of the other, both in prosperity and adversity.

The use of the word 'nature' is here ambiguous. It could be taken to mean *either* the characteristic and normative form of marriage *or* its determinative and invariable essence. Both views have been held and expressed by loyal and informed churchmen.

153.   With regard to divorce and remarriage the discipline and practice of the Church of England have likewise varied. At the Reformation the Church inherited the old canon law, under which the ecclesiastical courts, which had the jurisdiction in matrimonial cases, had the authority to declare a marriage null and void or to grant separation, but not to grant divorce with the right to remarry. The report of the Commission appointed by Edward VI (*Reformatio legum ecclesiasticarum*) recommended the acceptance by Church and State of the continental Reformers' views on marriage and divorce; but with the death of the king these proposals for change were allowed to lapse. However, it was possible to obtain a divorce, if not through the ecclesiastical courts, then by private act of Parliament; and up until 1857, when Parliament abolished the ecclesiastical jurisdiction in matrimonial cases, set up a civil court and legalised divorce on the ground of adultery,[1] 317 divorces were obtained in this way in England. These divorces were normally followed by remarriage in church. During the same period Canon 107 of the Canons of 1604 confirmed the authority of the ecclesiastical court to grant a judicial separation, but only on condition that the parties gave a definite pledge not to contract a second marriage.

154.   By and large the Church of England accepted the Act of 1857 since its legalisation of divorce on the ground of adultery was covered by the Matthaean exception.

155.   In the resolutions of the Lambeth Conference of 1888 it was declared that, in view of the teaching of Jesus, the Church could not recognise divorce in any case other than those of fornication or

---

[1]See Appendix 7, p. 174.

adultery. Even in these cases the guilty party should not have his remarriage blessed by the Church during the lifetime of the innocent party. As for the innocent party the Lambeth Fathers declared: 'That, recognising the fact that there has always been a difference of opinion in the Church on the question whether our Lord meant to forbid marriage to the innocent party in a divorce for adultery, the Conference recommends that the clergy should not be instructed to refuse the sacraments and other privileges of the Church to those who under civil sanction are thus married'. In the Conference of 1908 the same resolutions were affirmed, but it was added that 'when an innocent person has by means of a court of law divorced a spouse for adultery, and desires to enter into another contract of marriage, it is undesirable that such a contract should receive the blessing of the Church'. Put together, these resolutions allow the *possibility* of divorce and remarriage in church by the innocent party, but affirm its undesirability.

156.   At the beginning of the present century, according to Dr Winnett, 'a significant change occurred in Anglican opinion on divorce and remarriage, and took the form of a strengthening of the indissolubilist position'.[1] Dr Winnett attributes this change to the influence of biblical criticism in questioning the authenticity of the Matthaean exception, to the growth in Anglo-Catholicism and hence the resurgence of the Western tradition of moral theology, and to the increase in the number of divorces with their apparent threat to the institution of marriage and the resultant need for the Church to be uncompromising in repelling this threat. Thus, we note, considerations both of doctrine and of discipline were alleged to be pointing in the same direction.

157.   As the twentieth century has proceeded both the doctrinal and the disciplinary debates have continued. In the Church of England the view expressed in the 1908 Lambeth Conference resolutions was officially adopted by Resolutions in the Canterbury and York Convocations, most recently in 1957, though without committing the Church to the doctrine of indissolubility; and these govern the practice of the Church today (see para 5 for the text of the 1957 Resolutions). Nevertheless, in many ways the trend which was noticeable at the beginning of the century seems now to be reversing.

---

[1] *The Church and Divorce*, p. 7.

Several provinces within the Anglican Communion have already amended their discipline so as to allow, in certain carefully defined cases, remarriage in church. In so amending their discipline they have implicitly rejected the doctrine of indissolubility. As we have seen in Chapter 1, the Church of England has during the past decade been invited to follow their lead.

158. If we too find the doctrine of indissolubility untenable, as most of us on this Commission do, we have still to decide on the Church's discipline. What must be our faithful witness to our Lord? What action can we take to meet the needs of individual men and women whose marriages have broken down, which is at the same time consistent with our desire to strengthen the institution of marriage for the benefit of all, and with our Christian understanding of marriage as a life-long relationship?

159. We consider and set out possible answers to these questions in the next chapter of this Report. Before embarking upon that task, however, we need to look at the implications for the character of the marriage-contract, as Christians understand it, of the possibility of marrying a second time in the lifetime of a former partner. What is the significance of the fact that a couple marrying make an unconditional promise?

ARE THE PROMISES BINDING?

160. When it is held, as in traditional Roman Catholic teaching, that a marriage, once it has been duly ratified and consummated, cannot in any circumstances, at least if the partners are baptised Christians, be dissolved except by death, the conviction stems from what is believed to be the case concerning the nature of the bond itself. The power of the Church to dispense from vows, and the power of individuals to release each other from promises which they have made to each other, are beside the point. These powers are in certain circumstances indisputable. But where marriage is concerned—a contract between two persons which Christ is believed to have raised to a sacrament—these powers cannot be invoked. The marriage contract establishes the marriage bond, and this bond is in the order of things indissoluble. Thus it is the nature of what is contracted which makes the contract absolutely binding; it is not simply the contracting as such. When, however, a doctrine of the absolute indissolubility of the marriage bond is rejected, then attention is likely to focus on the nature of the moral obligation incurred by the mutual

promises, not least when these are described, as they are in the Book of Common Prayer, in terms of a 'vow and covenant'.

161. In speaking of marriage 'vows' we are undoubtedly giving the promise a seriousness and sacredness of the deepest kind possible. These vows are made by the couple each to the other. They are made in the presence of God, but they are not made directly to God. Unbelievers could equally well invest the marriage promises with a seriousness and sacredness which in their eyes justified their descriptions as 'vows', even if they did not believe in a God to whom religious vows could be made.

162. Marriage, as we have seen, is a contract; but it is more than a contract. It effects a status. The status established by the marriage contract is a social, not simply a private, affair. If it is to be terminated, it has to be terminated by the representatives of society; it cannot be terminated at will. According to the existing law of the land society recognises that the marriage status can be terminated in cases of irretrievable breakdown. In certain cases consent may be taken as sufficient evidence of such breakdown. This, however, is different from allowing a couple to terminate their marriage simply by registering their agreement so to do.

163. From a moral point of view the marriage contract has a further significance. The promises are more than the giving and receiving of certain rights. They are pledges of commitment. They establish a continuing relationship. They are unconditional in the sense that they initiate a covenant which no subsequent condition is to be allowed to break. The covenant is to be a covenant of loyalty and love, of sharing and caring, of cherishing and sustaining, exclusive and for life. It is to be for the giving and receiving of a personal identity within a shared personal world.

164. Suppose, however, that the relationship, far from creating a bond of love, becomes destructive and ceases to express the purposes for which the marriage covenant exists. Suppose the marriage is judged to have irretrievably broken down. Suppose, furthermore, as most of us are prepared to admit, that the marriage bond is thereby dissolved and that it is in the power of the civil courts to recognise this fact. In this case what moral force do the promises continue to have? They can no longer be kept in their fullness. Can they be kept in part by doing all in one's power to prevent a civil divorce? If moral

obligation does not extend thus far, can it require that, even when a civil divorce has taken place, no second marriage should be contracted? Or, when, humanly speaking, there is no possibility of reconciliation and the rebuilding of the relationship, does one have to admit that the fulfilment of ends which the promises had in mind is now no longer possible, and that the obligation which the promises originally imposed has now ceased to exist?

165. On this point moral judgements may differ. However, because most of us believe that the purpose of the promises is to establish, protect and deepen the marriage relationship, and because we accept the possibility of an irretrievable breakdown of that relationship and the dissolution of the marriage bond, we also accept the view that, when the bond has been dissolved, the promises no longer oblige in any part, and those who made those promises are henceforth free to enter into a second marriage. This is not to question the value and validity of the decision of those who refuse to enter into a second marriage, whether because of a continuing love for their former partner, or from regard for a relationship which once existed and which no other could replace, or for a witness to the character of the institution of life-long marriage as such. At the same time it is to affirm the consistency and integrity of those who feel able in all conscience to make identical promises of life-long commitment to a second person while the original partner to whom they made the promises in the first instance is still alive.

166. However, there is another matter to be considered. Even supposing that the truth of what is argued in the preceding paragraph is generally accepted, the question still remains whether the effect of allowing identical promises to be repeated is to cast doubt on the very meaning of these promises. Can they really be taken to mean what they seem to mean if it is possible to repeat them to another person during the lifetime of the person to whom they were originally made? Even if personal integrity is not incompatible with the repetition of identical promises, what of personal credibility? And what then of the social credibility and currency of the words in use? These questions do not directly raise ethical or theological issues. The issues are linguistic and social. But they are nonetheless important for that. The principle at stake is clear. The meaning of a promise is not immediately affected if on the exceptional occasion the promise is broken or becomes

impossible of fulfilment. But if the exceptions significantly increase, then the promise begins to lose its force as a promise; and the commitment which the words once expressed becomes a different commitment with a different meaning. Thus we have to ask whether it is possible, in the social conditions which actually obtain, to make it convincingly clear to one and all, when a person marries after divorce and makes the same promises for a second time, that this is an exception to the rule, that these promises remain unconditional and that marriage is for life.

167. From a Christian point of view marriage vows are made explicitly in the presence of God. Those entering upon a marriage set their life and love together within the context of the divine love. They offer themselves to God. They look to him as the source of an eternal love which draws all men to itself.

168. When such a marriage breaks down, there cannot but be an added sense of failure in discipleship to Jesus Christ and in response to the grace of God. As there were no vows made directly to God, it does not seem to us appropriate that the Church should be asked to pronounce any formal dispensation, even in cases in which it is persuaded that the promises, incapable of fulfilment, no longer oblige. On the other hand, the Church has a pastoral ministry to offer; and in ways in which it thinks fitting it will offer men and women the resources of forgiveness and renewal with which it has been entrusted.

CONCLUSION
169. In bringing this chapter to an end we wish to affirm once again a 'high' doctrine of marriage for both Christian and non-Christian. While most of us on the Commission cannot accept the doctrine of the absolute indissolubility of the marriage bond, we all believe that marriage 'intends' indissolubility and that many marriages achieve indissolubility. To repeat words which we have used before (para. 100), 'indissolubility is characteristic of marriage as it should and can be'. Such indissolubility is experienced, not as restriction and constraint, but as liberation and fulfilment. For such indissolubility is the fruit and culmination of a love which has learned to give everything and to receive everything. Marriage makes great demands; it also offers great joy.

170. Nevertheless, we are aware that marriages can and do break

down. Our understanding of the Christian doctrine of marriage does not lead us to condemn without more ado either divorce or marriage after divorce. Dissolution of the marriage bond is not an outright impossibility. Marriage after divorce is not necessarily a sin. The sin lies in the breakdown of the marriage, whether it is the deliberate sin of wickedness or the disorder of failure and muddle for which responsibility is hard if not impossible to assign.

171.   In these circumstances the Church has, we believe, a dual task, albeit rooted in a single conviction about marriage. In its ministry to individuals, married couples and families it must seek to help as many as possible to discover the riches of married love. In discharging this task it will regard as natural allies all those persons and organisations which exist to strengthen the institution of marriage and to support married people. It must also, as much through the quality of its pastoral care as through the terms of its formal regulations concerning remarriage, demonstrate the reality of its concern for those who have failed to realise the potentialities and meet the demands of married life. In all that it does it must take account of the actual social conditions in which its ministry to individuals and witness to society have to be conducted; in all that it does it must witness faithfully to the demand *and* the compassion of its Lord.

172.   In working out its total ministry it should bear in mind the needs both of Christians and of non-Christians. Marriage, in its characteristic form, is the same for both, a life-long and exclusive covenant. It belongs to the order of creation. In marriage men and women, whether Christians or not, can learn something of the heights and depths of love and, even unknowingly, can respond to the touch of the Spirit of God.

173.   Where people consciously make their marriage vows before God and set their married life within the context of the life and community of Christ's Church, we may confidently hope and expect that they will draw upon the many means of the divine love and mercy in deepening and strengthening their own relationship. In doing so, however, they are exempt neither from weakness nor from sin. In establishing a godly discipline for its own members the Church must not substitute the demands of law for the calling of grace.

4
The Task Before Us

'. . . to report on the courses of action open to the Church in seeking to promote in contemporary society the Christian ideal of marriage as a life-long union between husband and wife.'

174.   In the last chapter we pointed to the task facing the Church of England: what kind of marriage discipline it can develop which will help those who are about to marry or who are married to discover the full riches of married love, while ministering to the particular needs of those whose marriages have broken down and who may be seeking to remarry. The duty of the Commission is to report on the courses of action open to the Church as it seeks to carry out this task. The courses of action will be judged by their faithfulness to what Christians have perceived about the true character of marriage, and their aptness to meet the needs of contemporary society.

175.   In studying the understanding of marriage in contemporary society we have been made aware of three things in particular. First, marriage is still accompanied, in public attitudes as well as in the eyes of the law, by an expectation that it will be life-long and exclusive. This is as true of the increasing number of people who marry again following divorce as it is of those marrying for the first time. Second, there has been a major transformation in the relationship within marriage between husband and wife. Each of the partners now expects to find personal fulfilment and emotional satisfaction within marriage. Both in law and social convention substantial changes are taking place, bringing about a situation where husband and wife are regarded as equals. The longer life-expectancy of the couple, the freedom which contraception gives them to limit and space their family, and changing views on the roles of husband and wife, have all contributed to the contemporary view of marriage. Third, the very marked increase in the divorce rate in the 1960s and 1970s, though not susceptible as yet of any clear explanation, is likely to reflect the unstable position of many marriages, where the partners have high expectations of the relationship but little support from social attitudes or wider family or neighbourhood links.

176. This combination of high expectations of the marriage relationship, personal autonomy, and freedom to end unsatisfactory relationships is distinctive of our own day, and creates particular moral problems for society as a whole. In 1972 the late Bishop Ian Ramsey, speaking to the British Medical Association, pointed out the responsibilities which each new advance in freedom brings:

> A society which needs moral reform has for that reason never the moral stamina which the moral reform necessarily demands. If society had the moral stamina which a reform demands, the reform would not be necessary, it would happen naturally. This means that every moral reform has to be accompanied by a deepening of moral insight, and far from the Church or other institutions condemning liberalising laws, what they ought to be doing, more positively, is to be deepening moral insight, and in that way helping society to become morally more mature.

We believe that an effective Christian contribution to the situation facing our society in regard to marriage can be made, given the points of convergence between contemporary attitudes and the theological understanding of what marriage is.

177. In our theological chapter we stressed our conviction that marriage is first and foremost a personal relationship between one man and one woman, based on a free commitment to live and grow together. Marriage is to be seen primarily in personal and relational terms rather than in functional and social terms. While particular purposes served by marriage can be identified e.g. those listed in the Prayer Book marriage service, those purposes, and the roles they define, do not exhaust the meaning of marriage. This understanding of marriage has a lot in common with contemporary attitudes to marriage we have noted. It affirms that relationships are prior to roles. It is not a given role that determines the marriage relationship, it is the relationship which itself determines the roles.

178. We may, then, welcome those changes which make possible a greater freedom and depth of personal growth; for example, contraception liberates a wife from the role of continual child-bearing. On the other hand, change leads to instability; for where there are no universally recognised roles, expectations are uncertain and the building of a deep relationship becomes more difficult. Relationships need continual sustaining and renewing. The romantic view that they just happen is as wide of the mark as the view that they can be made to happen. If marriages are to last, then they must develop and grow as passing years lead from one stage to the next.

179.   Relationships necessarily develop roles and structures, even though these need not become fixed. Personal relationships require the support of social institutions. An emphasis on the purely private aspect of the marriage relationship may paradoxically weaken it: human beings need other forms of community for their full development. Marriage 'in the Lord' (I Cor. 7. 39) should tap deep resources of renewal and love, and at the same time prevent the marriage relationship from assuming the form of an idolatry.

180.   There is therefore both reinforcement for and challenge to contemporary attitudes to marriage in the Church's teaching. The Christian understanding equally emphasises 'what a man and a woman can become to each other and through each other, to their own mutual enrichment and to the enrichment of the larger community' (para. 82); but it points to the necessary context in 'a freely covenanted and life-long relationship of fidelity and love' (*ibid*). In its perfectness, marriage creates a bond which can properly be called ontological—real, permanent, with an objective existence. We are agreed that a marriage, once made, *ought* not to be broken. Some people would go further and affirm that it is in the nature of the ontological bond which marriage creates that it *cannot* be broken. Christians have a special responsibility to witness to the deepest needs and potentialities of human nature, in the light of the teaching of Jesus and its interpretation in the New Testament, supported by the living tradition of the Church. The teaching of Jesus, we believe, is clear: marriage is for life; husband and wife are one; divorce is as destructive of that unity as is adultery.

181.   When we come to consider the ministry of the Church we must be sensitive to the criticism that the Church is more interested in divorce than in marriage, and has appeared to speak at different times with different voices. At the same time we need to be clear that the Church's concern with the incidence of divorce, and with its own marriage discipline as it relates to divorced persons, stems from a real desire that the *institution* of marriage should not be damaged by any assumption that divorce is the normal response to strain and stress in marriage. If that were to come about not only would the Church's own pastoral ministry be made more difficult; the capacity of marriage as a relationship to elicit the best that human beings have it in them to become would be seriously weakened.

182. In what follows we do three things. We consider what the Church can do to strengthen the institution of marriage, and particular marriages, through its pastoral ministry and its involvement in society. We discuss specific problems relating to the Church's attitude towards people, including clergy, who have been divorced and who wish to remarry. Finally, we examine the question whether the Church of England should sanction the marriage in church of divorced persons. It should be said that in respect of each of these tasks what we are concerned with is a 'godly discipline', characterised by attention to the needs of individual people as well as for the health of the institution of marriage.

THE PASTORAL MINISTRY

183. The Church of England does not exercise its pastoral ministry in a void. In the way it ministers to individuals and married couples it is constrained by its desire to be obedient to Christ's teaching about marriage as it interprets that teaching. The Church must witness to its understanding of marriage as part of the God-given natural order, as a relationship which is life-long and exclusive.

The Social Context

184. The Church also has responsibilities in society deriving from the part it plays in solemnising marriages. Not only the Church of England, as the established Church, but all the major British churches share in the making of marriage-contracts as in other *rites de passage* marking crucial turning-points in people's lives, such as baptisms and funerals. The evidence suggests that during the past decade there has been a discernible turning away from the churches by those marrying for the first time. Nevertheless, although the proportion of marriages in church may have fallen, the Church continues to reach a remarkably high proportion of couples seeking to marry, with all that this affords in terms of pastoral opportunity. This responsibility, extending far beyond those who are regular churchgoers, is one of the primary means by which the Church 'promotes in contemporary society the Christian ideal of marriage'.

185. It has been possible for the Church to continue to exercise this responsibility in a rapidly changing society because there has not been any significant divergence in the understandings of marriage held in Church and State. As we saw in considering the law on marriage,

English law continues to regard marriage as in its inception a life-long union. Suggestions have been made from time to time that recent reforms in the law on divorce have wittingly or unwittingly so altered the law on marriage that it could no longer be said to be life-long. We have examined the evidence for such a change, and found it unconvincing. A situation could arise where the State's legislation so far diverged from Christian teaching as to make marriage as Christians understand it impossible to achieve legally. That situation has not so far arisen, and we reject utterly the contention that it has not been possible since 1969 for a Christian to marry on terms consistent with the teaching of the Church. Marriages under English law, whether solemnised in church or in a register office, are valid marriages according to traditional Church understanding.

186.   Proposals have, however, been made to us which do not depend upon a particular view of the law but which would nevertheless have the effect of putting the Church at a greater distance from the State than it is at present. Some people think that, in a situation in which the society in which we live is multi-racial and multi-cultural, the time has come to adopt the system, common in many other European countries, of universal civil marriage followed by a religious ceremony where the couple desire it. This arrangement, it is argued, makes functional sense. The State has a proper interest in the marriage of its citizens, since this will affect the status in law of the two parties and of any children they have, with all the legal rights and duties which follow. On the other hand, this system enables the couple to set their marriage in the particular religious and cultural tradition to which they belong, with all that this implies for themselves and their families in terms of the spiritual strength which it will bring.

187.   We understand that in countries where this system obtains, the civil marriage generally precedes the church marriage, but both ceremonies are, or purport to be, the marriage. The same pattern obtains in the handful of cases in this country where a couple wish to have the religious ceremony in an unlicensed building e.g. a college or school chapel. Many of us find a difficulty in this. In our Anglican understanding, marriage before a civil registrar is unquestionably marriage. All that remains to be done is for the marriage to be blessed—and we think it wrong that the couple having once exchanged the vows should go through the ceremony again. All of us

find the 'functional' argument unsatisfactory, since it appears to make a false distinction between the interests of the community and the interests of the Church. The Church is properly and necessarily concerned with the well-being of individuals and with their part in, and contribution to, the well-being of the whole community. We recognise that we live in a multi-racial and multi-cultural society. That does not reduce the responsibilities of the Church, though it certainly modifies the way they are carried out. The loss to the Church's pastoral outreach, were it to withdraw from the responsibility of sharing with, and in many instances acting for, the State in the solemnisation of marriages, would in our judgement far outweigh any possible gains.[1]

188.   One likely effect of the introduction of universal civil marriage would be a reduction in the number of marriages solemnised in churches and chapels. An alternative suggestion tending to the same result is that the Church should be able to refuse to allow the marriage in church of couples neither of whom is a committed Christian. This course of action, to be implemented, would require legislation since it would make an inroad into the citizen's common law right to be married in the church of the parish in which he or she lives. It would not be an easy course to apply, since it would involve the exercise of discretion by the parish priest in deciding who might be married in church and who might not.

189.   Some of those who have pressed this latter course upon us see it as an element in a broad pastoral strategy applying to other *rites de passage*. Its purpose would be to seek to mark off the committed from the uncommitted—and to give a new and sharper meaning in our society to what is involved in following Christ. Others approach the matter more particularly from their understanding of the nature of marriage. They feel that the standard which the Church sets and which is implicit in the marriage service—whether the indissolubilist position is maintained or not—is such that it is unreasonable to require people who are not Christians to accept it. Equally, it seems to be a mockery for a couple who are not practising Christians publicly

---

[1]In 1973, the Law Commission published a Report on *The Solemnisation of Marriage*, advocating universal civil preliminaries to marriage, while rejecting universal civil marriage on the grounds that public opinion would be against it. Evidence submitted to the Law Commission on behalf of the Church of England (published as GS Misc. 25) opposed even this limited alteration.

to be appearing to seek the blessing of God upon their union. If Church marriage were restricted to practising Christians, the argument runs, fewer of the marriages solemnised in church would be broken by divorce.

190.   We have no enthusiasm either for the suggestion that marriage in church should be restricted to the committed or for other courses which would involve 'distancing' the Church from the State. It seems to us that if the Church wishes, as our terms of reference say, 'to promote in contemporary society the Christian ideal of marriage', it will be better placed to do this if it maintains its traditional partnership with the State in the solemnising of marriages. We think that the Church would be acting contrary to the best interests of the society in which we live if in present circumstances it were to encourage the notion—implicit in the courses described in paras. 186 and 188—that there are two standards of marriage—a 'high' (or Church) standard and a 'low' (or Register Office) standard.[1]

191.   The fact that the State's law on marriage and the Church's understanding coincide does not mean that there are no grounds for disquiet. Although most couples are willing to accept preparation for marriage by a parish priest, and indeed do not enter upon marriage 'lightly or wantonly', the fact that the Church is established does involve the solemnising of a minority of marriages which may be deemed 'unadvised'. It is open to debate whether the lowering of the age at which a marriage can be contracted without the requirement of parental consent from 21 to 18 was altogether wise, in view of the widespread belief that teenage marriages are more at risk than those contracted later. Nonetheless, while there must be some safeguards against human frailty, we doubt whether it should be the Church which erects them. The promoting of a healthy view of marriage by Church and society seems a more positive approach.

National Policies
192.   Legal provisions alone however do not define the reality of marriage as people experience it; just as important are the policies and decisions of Government and other public bodies. The Church must be attentive to the bearing of these on healthy marriage and

---

[1]We discuss the related matter of the marriage of the unbaptised in paras. 275-83 below.

family life if it is adequately to discharge its responsibilities in society. Here we draw attention to two matters only, because of their particular importance. We would press the Church to take up each with Government as a matter of urgency.

193. First, then, we point to the continuing housing shortage, particularly of rented property, in many parts of the country; this has had a most serious effect on the ability of young married couples to set up house. In addition, municipal housing policies in some areas have tended to erode family life by creating large urban residential districts limited to two-generation families and by making it difficult for grown-up children to settle on the same estate as their parents.

194. Secondly, there is a curious discrepancy at the level of public policy-making, between an increasing awareness of the need for concerted policies for the *family*, and an almost total lack of interest in sustaining *marriages*. With the possible exception of the limited public funds channelled to marriage counselling agencies, there is next to no sign that Government values marriage as an important social institution. This cannot but have an impact in time on general public attitudes and on the expectations with which particular couples enter upon marriage. It must indeed be said that there is a lack of consistency between policies bearing on family life. We urge the need for intensive study within Government, whether by existing Departments, the Central Policy Review Staff or by a new agency acting as a centre of advocacy for marriage and family affairs, of the impact of government policies on married couples and families, who make an indispensable contribution to social well-being.

Pastoral Care
195. The Church's most far-reaching involvement with married couples takes place when couples are preparing for the wedding. We wonder if the general public, and indeed all members of the Church, realise how much time and trouble most of today's clergy take over the preparation of couples for marriage. They would not need to be reminded, as were their predecessors of 50 years ago by the 1920 Lambeth Conference, that it is part of their pastoral duty. They welcome the contact it gives them with young people, many of whom they will already know from Sunday school, confirmation class or youth club; and the preparation they give is seldom just a quick

69

run-through of the service but covers many aspects of the marriage relationship.

196.   We cannot however be entirely satisfied with the position which exists today. Many urban parishes are so large that a single-handed priest could not possibly have the time for adequate preparation of the number of couples he is called upon to marry. In addition, marriage counselling, whether undertaken as 'preparation' or to meet the needs of people already married, is a skill which needs to be acquired by study and practice; it is not conferred by ordination and indeed not all clergy are able to acquire it. We are not satisfied that sufficient attention is being given to the importance of training in this part of the clergyman's task. Training for counselling in marriage and family life should be regarded as an essential part of the courses offered in theological colleges and diocesan training schemes. We feel strongly however that parish clergy should regard marriage preparation as a task to be shared with others. In any group of clergy there will usually be one or two who are either particularly fitted or trained for this ministry. It should not be regarded as an infringement of another priest's rights if they undertake this work on behalf of the group.

197.   The work of the clergy in this area is complemented by the contribution which laypeople can make, particularly where the latter bring specialised skills. There are many valuable training projects in which laypeople are involved with the clergy, often with the encouragement, help and participation of local Marriage Guidance Councils. Concern for the stability of marriage must be seen to be a shared one, and not purely or mainly one for the clergy to exercise. We are aware of imaginative schemes which are in existence in many parts of the country. They may be designed mainly for engaged couples, or may include newly-marrieds as well. Usually they meet in small groups, and the sharing of experience and difficulties with other couples can be an enriching and liberating process. Subjects for discussion range from cash to sex. In addition to qualified marriage counsellors, there are experts in most communities who are willing to give of their time and knowledge in particular fields.

198.   In considering preparation for marriage it must be realised that it cannot be done in a few sessions a few weeks before the wedding day. Right attitudes cannot be developed in so short a time;

nor is a couple very likely to have 'second thoughts' when all the arrangements will have already been made months previously. Marriage preparation is a long-term process. It starts from a child's impression of the quality of his parents' marriage. Most people have been provided with a model of how husbands and wives relate to each other. The model may be followed, it may be modified or discarded: either way it exercises its influence, linking the generations. The Church has in the past century, mainly through the work of the Mothers' Union, endeavoured to give attention to the importance of the family as a training ground for the marriages of the next generation. We wish also to draw attention to the booklet *Marriage and the Family in Britain Today*, a survey by the General Synod Board for Social Responsibility,[1] which deals with the whole subject concisely but fully. A Church which is still predominantly organised on the basis of a ministry to people in their residential settings does not lack constant opportunities for encouragement, advice and help. Awareness of such opportunities can be taught to a congregation—whether expressed, for instance, in a well-organised system of parish visiting, or in the formation of a pressure group to influence the local community.

199.   A parish or a deanery which organises itself to take seriously the training of its families will not lack opportunity: yet it has to be admitted that many children and young people will inevitably not be touched by such efforts, however well directed. The Church of England has the opportunity—and the responsibility—to call the State's attention to what is a matter of national concern. We are well aware of the pressure on the timetable of schools and colleges of further education; but we consider that Personal Relationships—by which we do not mean merely Sex Education—should be a normal part of an educational curriculum since it represents another essential element in the long-term process of preparation for marriage. It should not simply be left to the member of staff concerned with Careers or 'R.E.'—still less treated as 'first aid' for 'casualties', to be dealt with by the school's Counsellor. We wish to draw particular attention to the recent initiative of the General Synod Boards for Social Responsibility and Education in setting up a working party on education in personal relationships.

---

[1]CIO, 1974.

200.   We have already observed that the fashioning of a true union in marriage 'involves sacrifice as well as fulfilment, pain as well as delight' (para. 140). Dr Jack Dominian, who was a valued contributor to the report *Marriage, Divorce and the Church*, emphasised to us the importance of the first five years of marriage. It is clear that many marriages are in need of help during this period. Particularly in urban areas the rootlessness and mobility of modern society, involving often the loss of support of parents and friends, can only too easily lead to strain in relationships. And the arrival of the first child inevitably means a change for which not all husbands and wives are prepared. It is true that during the early days of a marriage a couple will not always welcome well-meaning attempts at friendship when they are properly carrying out the building of their new relationship. But even in the most unpromising situations neighbourliness can be cultivated. The Church is committed to it by the great commandment of its Lord to love one another, and has unrivalled opportunities and facilities for such cultivation.

201.   The request for the baptism of the first child is an opportunity of the utmost value for making contact with a family at a moment when it will be receptive to friendship and concern. Christian Initiation must be seen not just as concern for the Family of God, but also as concern by the Family of God for a human family; and therefore the local church—and not merely the parish priest—should be involved. Contacts established at such a time can be of immense value in the times of loneliness, depression or strain which often occur during the early years of parenthood. In this connexion parishes might consider setting up 'pram clubs' or other opportunities for mothers of young children to meet each other and get out of the home. If a local authority social worker or health visitor were able to spend some time simply circulating among those using the club this would provide a means of giving support for hard-pressed mothers beyond what ordinary friendliness makes possible. In many localities the church is the only body able to make premises available for play-groups. A congregation could decide to organise a baby-sitting service, specifically in order to help young couples to get out of the house together from time to time. And finally we should not overlook the opportunity which the regular worship of the local church affords, whether through preaching or through imaginative use of the liturgy, for reflecting upon and celebrating marriage and family life.

202. We have been aware of imaginative schemes for marriage education being organised in some areas; two examples are given in Appendix 6. These show what can be done by the Church, often in collaboration with secular agencies, to help people in all stages of married life to explore and enrich their marriages, and so to be better able to help those who are in difficulty.

203. The 'extended family', in which three or more generations lived under one roof at any one time, has not been common in this country for two or three centuries at least, though it lingered on into the present century in some parts of the country. There is some evidence today of a desire to secure the advantages of the extended family and obviate the isolation which many young couples with small children experience. The growth of communities of families—providing something of the strength of the kinship and neighbourhood support which has been a feature of our own culture in the past and of many others—is a new and possibly transitory phenomenon. It is significant in that it is an indication of the concern which many Christians feel about qualities of care and of life in community which need to be preserved in our society. Perhaps also it serves to remind us that the community of the local church should itself always be such a support.

204. All that we have said so far in this chapter is designed to help the Church to make its contribution to the stability of family life and the enrichment of people's marriages. The task is an urgent one, and the Church must determine not just to do better what it is doing already, but to devote time, thought, money and manpower to the training of its members to seize the opportunities which are under their hands. We wish to stress that this is a task in which the laity must be fully associated.

Supporting Marriages Under Stress
205. Some element of tension is as natural to marriage as it is to life. The crucial distinction is between those marriages where the partners are able to integrate it with the rest of their experience of marriage, and those marriages where for whatever reason it imposes stress upon the relationship. Whether a particular couple are able to cope may depend to a very large extent on the help they are able to obtain from outside the marriage. But marriages, in spite of all efforts to help, do

in fact break down, and are breaking down in ever larger numbers, as we have noted. The Church has a responsibility to those who are involved in such breakdowns—nor can we be blind to the fact that not a few of them are its own committed members. Indeed, the increased incidence of marriage breakdown among the clergy should alert us to the fact that the changes and developments in society in our time, which we have noted in Chapter 2, affect all alike.

206.   The nature of a priest's work in particular often subjects his marriage and his family to strain and stress, whether because the parsonage is 'open house' to the parish or because of the impossibly long hours which many clergy work. For this reason the quality of the marriage relationship of candidates for ordination needs to be carefully considered by those responsible for their selection and training; and in ordination and post-ordination training attention should be given to the priest's family life. We doubt whether bishops, archdeacons and rural deans need reminding of their pastoral duty in this direction; we draw attention to it since we consider that it has become more pressing of late and therefore deserves more study than it has up to now received.

207.   Counselling those facing marriage difficulties is a skill not easily learned. We commend the work of the National Marriage Guidance Council in providing a counselling service for those in marriage difficulties. We are in no doubt that Government and local authorities should recognise the value of its work by making available greatly increased financial support, and that members of the Church should offer themselves for training as counsellors, and co-operate with, and seek the co-operation of, the Council in the whole area of marriage counselling and preparation. We should also like to draw attention to the work of the Institute for Marital Studies in training counsellors, and hope that it may be possible for the Church to make full use of the facilities it offers. We await with interest the publication of the Home Office Consultative Document on Marriage Counselling. It is clear that any significant impact of such work on the incidence of marriage breakdown reflected in the figures for separation and divorce will only come about through imaginative developments in marriage counselling and effective collaboration among all the bodies concerned.

Divorce and Remarriage

208.   We have already posed the question what the Church can do, when a marriage has broken down, to limit the damaging consequences and promote future good. And we have set out what we believe to be the principles which must guide us in our answer to that question, in paras. 171-3.

209.   It has already been acknowledged that for most of us on the Commission 'our understanding of the Christian doctrine of marriage does not lead us to condemn without more ado either divorce or marriage after divorce . . . The sin lies in the breakdown of the marriage, whether it is the deliberate sin of wickedness or the disorder of failure and muddle for which responsibility is hard if not impossible to assign' (para. 170). Nevertheless divorce is itself almost always a traumatic experience. There is almost always a sense of failure, if not of guilt, and the Christian pastor has to deal with both. The first concern of the Church is, and must be, with the pastoral care and support of those concerned—husband, wife and children. Too often the Church has seemed censorious and lacking in compassion:.there is a task here not only for the clergy but also for laypeople. Some laypeople will have particular skills to put at the service of those of their friends and neighbours who are in need of help. But for many what is required is simply friendship and support in times of difficulty.

210.   In the exercise of these ministries, clergy and laypeople must be prepared to face the fact of divorce as an element in the life of the society in which we live. Amongst those whose marriages effectively break down there will still be some who will feel that, as Christians, they must witness to the Christian ideal by themselves refusing to initiate divorce proceedings. This view, sincerely held, must be respected, though many of us question whether it gets the emphasis right. For the individual, the other partner and the family, the decree of divorce and the associated order and agreements will provide a frame for the altered relationships. The conscientious individual may well witness more effectively to the position which he holds not by refusing or resisting the divorce but in his subsequent conduct—e.g. in relation to the decision whether or not to marry again.

Exclusion from Holy Communion

211.   Among those who are seeking to minister to those who have been divorced and who do decide to marry again, there is widespread

dissatisfaction with the existing discipline by which communicants who marry after divorce may be excluded for a period from Holy Communion. As we have noted, the 1888 Lambeth Conference recommended that clergy should not be instructed to refuse the sacraments to people in these circumstances. Nevertheless the practice appears to have spread as part of the process of the hardening of Anglican opinion against divorce and remarriage, and was codified in the resolutions of Convocation of 1938 and 1957. Anxiety about the use of exclusion in this way has been a feature of the recurring debate on the Church's marriage discipline in recent years (see Chapter 1).

212.   The Church's formularies envisage that anyone who is 'an open and notorious evil liver' is to be excluded from the Communion until he has repented of his ways. Where a marriage is under strain or where it breaks down, there may well be circumstances where the priest would be right to ask one or both parties not to present themselves as communicants, e.g. where one party was known to be living in adultery. The need for such action at this stage rarely arises, because in practice the person concerned voluntarily ceases to be a communicant. Under the Convocation regulations the question of exclusion from Communion arises only at a later stage, not as a direct response to divorce, but at the point when a person who has been divorced decides to remarry.

213.   We are all of us uneasy about the use of automatic exclusion at this point. There may well be cases of remarriage after divorce where it would be an open scandal for the parties to receive Communion and where it is right that they should be excluded. In general, however, as in the former case the 'evil liver' will resolve the matter by not seeking to communicate. But the Church's predominant concern must be with the pastoral care of those involved in divorce and remarriage; and we are anxious about the impact of exclusion in those cases, which we believe to be numerous, where a man or woman, conscious of and sorry for past failures, nevertheless conscientiously decides that it would be right to remarry. We are aware that the Convocation regulations are in fact set in the context of 'the preservation of the Church's witness to our Lord's standard of marriage and to the pastoral care of those who have departed from it'. We are also aware, as the Synod debates and our own enquiries revealed, that in recent years it has become more and more the practice to restore people to Communion very soon, if not immediately, after the marriage; and

76

that many bishops give high priority to their own pastoral responsibilities at this point, often meeting and talking with the couple about their future.

214. These considerations may mitigate what would otherwise be damaging consequences of the practice; they do not go to the heart of the matter, still less do they represent a justification for the practice. We consider that the negative use of the sacrament of Holy Communion, and of the grace which it affords, is unsatisfactory. Such a discipline is not a normal part of the Anglican tradition and should be used only in very extreme cases. To receive Communion is the sign that a person continues to be a member of the Church; it is not a certificate of personal righteousness, nor should it or any other means of grace be taken as such. By implication therefore, continued admission to Communion of a divorced and remarried person should not be treated as though it constituted a seal of approval on his or her action. On the other hand, those who marry after divorce with a sense of need of the grace of God should be given every assurance possible, by sacrament and prayer, of the heights and depths of the love of God. *We therefore recommend that the Convocation regulations requiring that those who marry after divorce should only be admitted to Communion with the permission of the Bishop should be rescinded.*

MARRIAGE IN CHURCH AFTER DIVORCE

215. So far we have considered the character of the Church's marriage discipline as it applies generally. In discussing the Church's response to those whose marriages break down and who marry a second time, we have not distinguished between those who choose to marry by civil ceremony and those who seek, successfully or unsuccessfully, to have their second marriage solemnised in church. In general the pastoral problems and opportunities facing the Church are the same in each case, though the Church is less well placed to establish contact with those who choose to marry by civil ceremony, unless they are also communicants. It is now, however, necessary to consider the character and extent of the problem facing the Church by reason of the desire of some to be married in church following divorce, and then to consider the courses of action open to the Church.

216. The present practice of the Church of England is governed by regulations of the Convocations of Canterbury and York. Under the

77

statute law of the land a parish priest has the right to marry in church persons who have already been married but whose previous marriage has been terminated by divorce.[1] But under resolutions of the Convocations the Church of England does not permit the use of the marriage service in the case of anyone who has a former partner still living. These regulations of the Convocations have no legal force but they have been regarded as having considerable moral authority. At the present time they are followed by most diocesan bishops and by the great majority of their clergy. But in recent years some clergy have felt free to disregard them, and to accede to requests by divorced persons to be married in church.

217.   It is impossible to find out the extent of the demand for remarriage in church since no records are kept of those requesting it. We have seen (para. 37) that in 1975 just under 500 marriages involving divorced people were solemnised by Anglican ceremonies. This admittedly small number represents both an absolute increase over earlier figures (1964, 62; 1970, 127), and an increase as a proportion of all remarriages.

218.   Though the figures suggest that, quantitatively speaking, remarriage in church is not a pressing problem for the Church of England, this does not dispose of the matter. Differences in practice between the Church of England and the Free Churches, and revised regulations concerning nullity now in force in the Roman Catholic Church, have led to the position that the Church of England now appears to have the strictest marriage discipline of all the churches in this country. Within the Church of England the past decade has been marked by increasing impatience among some clergy with the present rules, even where they continue to observe them. Evidence received from one diocese in the Midlands indicates that 50 per cent of the clergy in that diocese were dissatisfied with the present rule that they must refuse marriage in church to all divorcees. In two dioceses the diocesan bishop has made it known that he regards his clergy as free to marry divorced people in appropriate cases. In dioceses where the bishop continues to base his practice on the Convocation regulations, some clergy are willing 'to take the law into their own hands' or (more accurately) to exercise the right which the law of the State gives them. Nevertheless these cases are, as we have seen, still comparatively

[1]See Appendix 7, p. 176.

few—and where the bishop adheres to the Convocation regulations, the vast majority of clergy follow his lead. It should also be said that such evidence of dissatisfaction as we have cited above can be balanced by evidence from other dioceses which gives a somewhat different impression; it would be misleading to suggest that the clergy of the Church of England were as a whole dissatisfied with the present situation.

219. Over against those basically dissatisfied with the existing practice of the Church stand those who, on varying grounds, believe that it is essential that the Church should maintain its refusal to marry divorced persons in church. Some base their opposition on an 'indissolubilist' view of the marriage bond. Others, while acknowledging that marriages can and do break down and that second marriages may in practice display all the marks of a loving and caring relationship as Christians understand marriage, would still reject remarriage in church. They feel that it weakens the Church's witness to life-long marriage and cheapens its ceremonies if people are allowed to take the vows in church for a second time in the lifetime of the first partner. All those who are opposed to remarriage in church are anxious about the effect on public opinion in the wider community. If the Church of England withdraws from the position embodied in the Convocation regulations will not people draw the conclusion (whatever is said to the contrary) that the Church is weakening in its commitment to the Christian ideal? People who argue in this way do not wish to be thought lacking in compassion for those whose marriages break down. We have found, even amongst those who take the 'indissolubilist' positon, a reluctance to say that a person who has been divorced should in no circumstances remarry. Nor do they say that the second marriage is in such a case no marriage, though they will feel that it is 'something less than marriage in its fullness'. They are clear, however, that such a marriage should not take place in church. To those who would wish to marry in church but who cannot do so under present rules, they commend the thought that in this they bear their part in witness to the Christian ideal.

220. We have not thought it our duty to attempt to make an overall assessment of the strength of the various opinions in the Church of England. It is sufficient to say that all these opinions exist and have been strongly expressed to us. Our own duty is to report on 'the courses of action open to the Church' in this situation. We therefore·

set out in the remainder of this chapter what appear to us the courses facing the Church, and indicate our views upon each.

AN EXTENSION OF NULLITY

221. Some people who wish the Church of England to maintain its refusal to remarry divorced people in church, but who would like the Church to be able to take a more flexible position than is at present possible, have suggested that there may be a way forward by an extension of the concept of nullity, and they draw attention to recent developments in the Roman Catholic Church.

222. As we have explained in Chapter 2, it is open to the courts of the land to find that a marriage is null and void. If a marriage is declared a nullity by the law courts then in our practice and (as we understand it) that of the Roman Catholic Church, there is no objection to either party contracting another marriage—and (in either communion) that marriage can take place in church. We think that the Church of England should continue its present practice in this regard. The grounds of nullity as admitted by the courts are set out in para. 62. In Roman Catholic practice the Church itself establishes courts charged with the task of reviewing, from an ecclesiastical standpoint, certain decisions of the secular courts; and as time has gone on the Roman Catholic Church has enlarged its concept of nullity so that it is now a good deal wider than that which the English courts admit. The significance for individual Roman Catholics is that a man or woman who has been divorced (by the State) can then apply to the Church for a declaration that, in the Church's eyes, the marriage was null. If such a declaration is granted, the applicant is free to marry in church. An extended account of this jurisdiction appears in Appendix 2.

223. We do not think that this Roman Catholic practice offers a way forward which the Church of England could or should follow. The Roman Catholic authorities have enlarged the number of cases which can be regarded as null, chiefly by taking account of any evidence of what is described as 'psychological immaturity' in either or both of the partners at the time of the marriage. We can well see that such a system may be acceptable in a Church where it is a development from traditional doctrine and practice. We consider that, if it were to be transplanted suddenly into the life of the Church

of England, it would be regarded as an artificial way of dealing with the problems of marriage breakdown, and one bristling with practical difficulties of organisation and procedure. It would introduce a quasi-judicial process into an area of our Church's life where, at present, none exists; if there is to be development, we should prefer to see a pastoral rather than a legal procedure. Moreover, we would still be left with the pastoral problems which arise where undoubtedly valid marriages break down as a result of stresses and strains in the relationship of the couple in married life. We also think that it would be comparatively expensive in terms of the time and cost to those who would have to administer it, and to the applicants and their advisers.

224.   But there are theological and psychological objections as well as practical difficulties. We know of no general agreement among theologians, psychologists or the general public about what constitutes psychological maturity or immaturity in people of any age. In a fundamental sense all of us are engaged in a process of growing towards maturity throughout our lives and are necessarily immature at the outset of a relationship which makes such a significant contribution to that growth. That apart, there is something basically unsatisfactory in a procedure which calls into question the validity of a relationship which may have been in existence for many years. In an extreme case a marriage could be found to be null after, say, 25 or 30 or more years of cohabitation and after the production of a family. By contrast the traditional grounds of nullity tend to be apparent fairly soon after the ceremony, with non-consummation as the most generally identified ground. It is also inequitable to allow relief on the ground of immaturity *at the time of marriage* but not in respect of subsequent immaturity; emotional immaturity may mark people's relationships at any age. It is important to remember that nullity is essentially a judicial process: the law allows that there are certain identifiable circumstances in which it could be said that a particular marriage was no marriage. But we have to distinguish these cases, likely at all times to be few, from the broader range where it is possible to say that a marriage was doomed from the outset because the partners rushed into it 'unadvisedly, lightly or wantonly'. Some of us may say of the latter 'there never was a real marriage'. But this does not mean that the appropriate relief is, or ever should be a decree of nullity—which, in many cases, could only be a pretence. For all these reasons therefore we reject the suggestion that the Church of England should adopt an extended understanding of nullity.

225.   Many clergy who adhere to the Convocation regulations forbidding remarriage in church nevertheless recognise that some at least of those who seek to be married in church following a divorce wish for an opportunity to pray together and to dedicate themselves at the beginning of the new marriage. Private services of prayer and dedication frequently take place, either in the couple's home or in church, and the existence of such services is explicitly envisaged, if not formally sanctioned, by the Convocation regulations. In addition public services are held by some clergy which in greater or lesser degree resemble the marriage service.

226.   It has been put to us that the provision of an officially-approved form of service of prayer and dedication would go far to meet the needs of some of those marrying after divorce while preserving the Church's distinctive witness to the permanence of marriage.

227.   There are Christians who believe that it is right and godly for them to enter into a second marriage after the first has been legally dissolved and while the previous partner is still alive. Their decision to remarry is their own, made after due reflection and prayer, and made in good conscience. They believe that God is calling them to this second marriage. They are willing to acknowledge that divorce and remarriage falls short of what God intends, and that in an age when many are rejecting the norm of life-long, exclusive monogamy it is prudent and right that the Church should witness to this norm by refusing to remarry anyone who has been divorced and whose partner is still living. Nevertheless, they seek for more than the priest's private prayers said with them either in church or at home. They seek

(1)   a means of grace to encourage them along the path which they have chosen;

(2)   an opportunity for sharing their discovered vocation with their friends and neighbours in humility, wonder and joy;

(3)   an acknowledgement of the mercies of God within the family of Christ and of the continuing fellowship and acceptance of one another in the Church.

228.   A service of blessing and dedication would not be a marriage, and would contain no marriage vows. The couple would come to church as a married couple, or before their marriage. The service

would express penitence for the past, thanksgiving and joy in the present and dedication for the future. In all such expression the Church would, as the Body of Christ, be associated. It would not be expressing its approval *or* its disapproval of the marriage, though in providing this service rather than a marriage service, it would be retaining its witness against divorce and remarriage in general and in the abstract. The use of such a service could be left to the discretion of the parish priest, but he would still be acting in the name of the Church.

229.　In favour of this suggestion it could be argued that it would meet a pastoral need which is difficult legally to meet at present. Such a service could also be used if the Church were to alter its existing marriage discipline so as to permit the marriage of divorced persons in church in certain circumstances; the service would be available for those who either did not want remarriage in church or were unable to obtain it. The existence of such a service would incidentally also dispose of the problem, noted in para. 187, where for any particular reason two people marrying for the first time have to have a civil marriage followed by the use of the marriage service in church.

230.　We nevertheless see fundamental objections to the suggestion. We believe that there would be a continuing risk of confusion between the service proposed and the marriage service. It has already been noted that some clergy offer a form of service which closely resembles the marriage service (para. 225). Even if the minister had carefully explained the difference between a service of dedication and a marriage service to the couple, it is likely that some of those taking part in the service would be unaware of the distinction. This risk would be increased if, as seems likely, elements of the traditional ceremonial associated with a wedding appeared in the service. The appearance of the bride in white, the ringing of bells, the wedding march—all these would convey a powerful though misleading message which the words of the service would be unable to correct.

231.　No minister could be compelled to take such a service. In practice the clergy would come under considerable pressure to make the service available to all who asked for it, since a couple who were denied the use of an official service of the Church would regard this as a mark of disapproval or rejection. If however the service became widely used, there would be a risk of confusion between this service and the marriage service, and it would be difficult for the Church to dispel the impression that it had begun to remarry all comers.

232. We are therefore of one mind in rejecting the suggestion of a public service of prayer and dedication. *We recommend that the present use of such services should be brought to an end.* Their use is liable to convey the impression that a marriage is taking place, particularly where such services approximate to the marriage service.

THE CHOICE FACING THE CHURCH

233. The extension of nullity and the provision of a public service of prayer and dedication are both in their different ways attempts to meet a particular problem by bypassing the Convocation regulations. We have come to the conclusion that a solution is not to be sought along those lines. In our view the Church is faced with a choice between two possible courses of action:

(a) to maintain the present official position that divorced persons should in no circumstances be married in church[1]; and

(b) to adopt a system whereby, without conceding a general right of remarriage in church, divorced persons were in certain cases permitted to be married in church following a pastoral enquiry.[2]

There is in theory a third possible course, namely that all divorced persons who wish to be married in church should be allowed to do so. No-one has come forward in evidence to argue in favour of this, nor do we think it represents a realistic course for the Church to entertain. We therefore do not consider it further.

(i) *No remarriage in church*

234. The first of the two courses of action can be simply stated, though it does not represent merely the continuation of the present situation. If the Church decided after debate to maintain the position that divorced people should not be married in church it would not be sufficient to 'do nothing', since it is dissatisfaction with the existing system which has caused two successive enquiries to be set up. It would therefore be necessary for that decision to be formally affirmed by the General Synod, and embodied in an Act of Synod. Thereafter, all clergy, including those who do not at present adhere to the existing

---

[1]Four members of the present Commission support this course.
[2]Twelve members of the present Commission support this course.

84

Convocation regulations, would be expected to accept and loyally to implement it.

(ii) *Remarriage in church in certain cases*

235. The second of the two courses of action we have identified would also represent a departure from existing practice. As things stand at present, the parish priest is free in law to marry divorced people at his discretion. In our judgement the use of this liberty is inconsistent with the maintenance of a clear witness to the Church's general teaching on the permanence of marriage. For any scheme of selective remarriage to work, it must be clear that the occasions when remarriage in church occur are exceptional and determined by a consistent policy. The only way to ensure that this happens is to require that the decision in each case be taken by the bishop, or by members of a small panel nominated by the bishop to act on his behalf. In taking this view we differ from the Root Commission, which considered that the responsibility for the decision should in each case rest with the parish priest concerned.

236. We set out in Appendix 5[1] a description of the way such a procedure might work. It is essential to the effectiveness of the procedure that the parish priest should forward particulars of every application to remarry in church to the bishop and be bound by his decision, subject to a right to refuse to solemnise a particular marriage or to allow his church so to be used. It would be necessary to embody the procedure in an Act of Synod replacing the existing Convocation regulations. We assume that it would be impracticable to seek to withdraw the statutory right of the parish priest to remarry at his discretion, but in this situation also all clergy would be expected loyally to implement the new rules.

237. If the Church were to adopt this course of action it would need to decide upon the form of service to be used in solemnising the marriage of divorced people. The choice would effectively lie between using one of the existing authorised services without alteration or one of those services but with a special Preface, or a special service. The Orthodox Churches traditionally use a different form of service for second and subsequent marriages, though we understand that in Western Europe at least contemporary Orthodox practice is to use the same service. A special service would be appropriate if the second

---

[1]See p. 162 below.

marriage were seen as fundamentally different in character from the first, but not otherwise. On the other hand, to use the ordinary service unaltered would be to suggest that there is no difference at all between the two cases.

238.   A distinction needs to be drawn between *modifications* to the existing service on the one hand, and *additions* to it on the other. It has been represented to us that it would be felt to be inappropriate for a person remarrying after divorce to use the same form of promise a second time—and that this feeling would be shared by at least some of those people themselves. Even if a change in the form of the promise for second marriages were acceptable to Parliament, it would still in our judgement be essential to resist any pressure for a different form of words: those coming to the Church to be remarried after divorce would need to be reminded as clearly as possible that the commitment they entered into was identical with that they undertook in the first marriage. It would however be necessary to add to the form of service a Preface declaring the circumstances of the marriage and the fact that diocesan permission had been given.

239.   The Root Commission envisaged that as part of the preparation for the remarriage of divorced persons, the priest would meet the couple some days before the date of the marriage, possibly in church, for a private occasion of prayer. 'In it', their Report states, the couple 'would give expression, first, of penitence for past faults; secondly, of their intention to meet those obligations which still remained; thirdly, of a right intention in the new marriage; and fourthly, of desire for God's renewing and recreative grace within which to live'.[1]

240.   We do not consider that an occasion of prayer such as they describe should be an element in a procedure for marrying divorced people in church. We think that the four matters to which they refer should be within the scope of the enquiry by the bishop or his representatives which would precede the granting of permission for the marriage in church. They would also have been considered in the pastoral interview which the priest would have had with the couple. We see little value in a further traversing of the same ground in the context of a private service, held after the diocesan decision had been taken.

---

[1]*Op. cit.*, p. 74.

241. Two things can be stated with confidence about both the courses of action we have identified. In the first place, the case for each is put forward by its exponents in the belief that it will strengthen the Church's witness to Jesus' teaching on marriage. The reader must therefore evaluate the contribution each will make to achieving this purpose without, however, isolating it from the other observations and recommendations contained in the Report. Secondly, just as there are dangers and disadvantages in the Church's existing discipline, so there are in the alternatives now proposed. We have sought to describe them accurately and fairly, but we are not agreed what weight to attach to each or all of them.

(i) *The case for remarriage in Church*

242. At the heart of the case for allowing divorced persons in certain cases to marry in church lie three convictions. First, the faith that marriage is essentially 'for life' must also reckon with the fact that marriages can and do break down and people can and do seek to start afresh in a new marriage. Second, one important reason for marriage breakdown is the heightened expectations with which couples today approach marriage. This changing understanding of marriage in our society presents the Church with a new challenge and a new opportunity in exercising its ministry. The situation in which the Church finds itself has also changed. For example, an increasing proportion of all marriages (not least those of people marrying for the first time) involves divorced people. Third, in these circumstances an invariable refusal to remarry in church leads many people to conclude that the Church regards the sin involved in the breakdown of marriage as the one sin which can never be forgiven. However far this conclusion may be from the truth, it cannot effectively be dispelled, and the Gospel of forgiveness cannot effectively be declared in word and action, so long as those conscientiously seeking the blessing of the Church on a subsequent marriage must be turned away.

243. Marriage is 'for life'. Both the logic of the unconditional commitment of love and Jesus' teaching on God's will in creation express this conviction. The commitment is real and binding from the moment when it is made; nevertheless, it is in the living relationship that the commitment is to be worked out and the union to be made. The making of this union affects the total being or character of each of the partners. Thereby it becomes an 'ontological' bond, and it can

truly be said to reveal the 'one-flesh' character of marriage, as the Bible speaks of it.

244.   For either partner to end the marriage and marry another is to destroy what was intended to be indestructible. Nevertheless, some marriages do break down. There may have been culpable sins of selfishness and neglect, or there may have been weaknesses and failures of personality in circumstances in which moral responsibility is difficult to identify. In this or that marriage it may no longer be possible to maintain the commitment of mutual cleaving and loving, and thus it becomes apparent that the marriage itself, considered as a relationship determined by this commitment, has come to an end. The issue of a decree of divorce is both a formal recognition of this state of affairs, and a rescinding of the marriage status. When this occurs one or both of the partners may wish to contract a subsequent marriage. In terms of the law they are free to do so. The Christian understanding of marriage does not compel us to say that they are still morally or spiritually bound to each other; though the commitment shaped each of the partners, so that they can never be the same as they were before they married, nevertheless the conditions in which it could still be fulfilled no longer obtain. Neither the promises nor the union which they brought into being has any continuing power to bind.

245.   Today an increasing number of people are finding themselves in this situation. They represent a steadily growing proportion of the total number of marriageable people, so that a person marrying for the first time is increasingly likely to choose as a spouse someone who has been married before. This does not represent a rejection of the institution of life-long marriage, though the incidence of breakdown and recourse to divorce undoubtedly give cause for concern. It does however present the Church with a challenge to its existing refusal to remarry divorced persons, since the group thus affected includes many people marrying for the first time, as well as others who are sincerely penitent for their part in the breakdown of an earlier marriage and who wish to make a new start with the assurance of God's forgiveness and the blessing of the Church. The partners are legally free to remarry. It must be asked whether the Church is morally free, while remaining loyal to the teaching of Jesus, to remarry them.

246. This teaching, while intended to be taken with the utmost seriousness, is not to be understood as Law. In the Gospel narratives there is evidence both of the challenge which Jesus' words about marriage and divorce created, and of the beginnings of the process by which the Church sought to remain faithful to them while at the same time developing a pastoral discipline appropriate to the situations in which people found themselves. This process has never ceased. Throughout history the Church has had to work out ways, not of weakening the impact and demand of the Gospel, but of proclaiming it as much in situations of failure and sin as when men and women have heard it gladly and responded to it without stumbling. Loyalty to Jesus Christ requires both stringency and compassion: the maintenance (in the context of marriage) of the high demand on those who marry that they commit themselves in love to each other for life, and the declaration of God's forgiveness of those who recognise their failure in meeting that demand and in good conscience seek his support in making a fresh start. Thus while the Church is free, and indeed bound, to respond compassionately to all who marry after divorce, not least to those who are practising members of the Church's life, its response to those who ask for remarriage in church should depend on evidence of penitence on the part of the divorced person, and of a realistic awareness of their own dependence on God's grace on the part of both the man and the woman. For this reason some procedure is required to establish whether such evidence exists. In order that the procedure and criteria followed may be substantially the same throughout the Church of England, it should be the diocesan bishop or his nominees who take the decision, rather than the incumbent on his own. Nevertheless, since what is involved is an exercise of a pastoral rather than a legal responsibility, the incumbent should be associated with the procedure as the couple's pastor, and every effort should be made to set it within the context of the Church's caring ministry for all married people, including those who remarry by civil ceremony.

247. The case for such a change has so far been discussed largely in terms of theological truth and pastoral appropriateness. It would, however, also represent a positive response to a shift in the understanding of marriage which has been characteristic both of social attitudes and of the law in our society in recent years. The principles and practices reflected in the marriage service were derived from a society in which marriage was under far tighter control and

support by religious, legal, governmental, neighbourhood and family institutions even than those characteristic of England during the times in which the Prayer Book was produced. Gradually during the last three or four hundred years, and very rapidly during the present century, the support and control of marriage given in all of these spheres has decreased until, today, marriage stands or falls by the quality of the relationship between the spouses. The emphasis on the development of this relationship, the search for mutuality and personal growth through marriage, the recognition that divorce is not so much a matter of allocating blame as a remedy for the utter breakdown of a relationship—all these factors have both derived from and contributed to religious thought, and represent points of convergence with much current Christian thinking about the nature of marriage. The Church's witness to the true character of marriage falls on ears ready to hear; but in its present refusal to remarry it immediately creates a barrier to understanding, and a sense of injustice, which on occasion lead to permanent alienation from the Church and in general perpetuate a belief that it is out of touch with the reality of married people's lives.

248.   The result of putting into practice the present proposals would be two-fold. In the first place the present crisis of conscience which many clergy experience, between obedience to the bishop and the Convocation regulations on the one hand, and the desire to do what seems pastorally required on the other, would be removed.

249.   In the second place, as far as the witness of the Church in society is concerned, the dangerous impression of pharisaism and unrealism which attends the existing discipline would be dispelled. It would be apparent that the Church's concern for the stability and permanence of people's actual marriages was being affirmed in a way which could have a stabilising effect on the institution of marriage itself. Instead of standing apart from men and women marrying after divorce and thus being unable to influence their attitudes and intentions as at present, the Church would be in a position to meet them where they are and to emphasise their need for a realistic awareness of the past and of a mutual commitment for the future. Although such a witness would not have the obvious simplicity of a refusal to remarry in any circumstances, it could in fact do more to support and strengthen the reality of individual marriages than the adoption of an exceptionless rule. Insistence on an exceptionless rule

may drive men and women to despair of reaching out to the goal which the very rule itself is intended to commend. By contrast the approach here advocated reflects the belief that 'there is still the opportunity to offer the world not a misty ideal but a reality so definite and so attractive that there is room for the generous acknowledgement of exceptions which are rightly given special treatment'.[1]

250. Nevertheless there are risks which must be acknowledged. Pastoral care, combining firmness with mercy, is never easy to exercise with wisdom and prudence. Furthermore, it might prove difficult to maintain the balance in the diocesan procedure between pastoral sensitivity and consistency of practice. This might lead to charges of unfairness. One could not be certain that the public, used to thinking of the Church as there to marry all and sundry, would grasp the reason for its refusal to remarry in general combined with a readiness to remarry on occasion. Finally, the fact that the clergy of the Church of England would be operating a procedure likely to be regarded by some as conceding too much to secular change, and by others as exposing the clergy to undesirable pressures from applicants (and their relatives) for remarriage might itself lead to inconsistencies in operation.

251. In the nature of the case it is impossible to say in advance how real such risks would prove to be. None of them represents a conclusive argument against the proposal being discussed. Attitudes, however, are likely to be at least as significant as procedures in determining how any new marriage discipline works out in practice.

(ii) *The case against permitting remarriage in Church*
252. Those who believe that the Church of England should maintain its present refusal to marry divorced persons in church do so for positive reasons and not simply because they are anxious about the practical consequences of a change. At the heart of their case is the belief that the refusal by the Church to give its public seal of approval to any marriage after divorce is essential if the Church's witness to marriage as involving an unconditional commitment is to be maintained. Not all of those who take this view ground it on belief in the indissolubility of the marriage bond.[2] Since however this belief represents the weightiest theological case against the view which

---

[1]Helen Oppenheimer, *The Marriage Bond* (Faith Press, 1976), p. 14.
[2]See Appendix 3, p. 123.

would in certain circumstances countenance remarriage in church, its bearing on remarriage is appropriately considered first.

253. 'The indissolubilist tradition in the Church maintains that marriage involves a moral commitment and a spiritual bond which are not merely a function of the empirical manifestations of marriage—shared home, sexual relationship, children, etc. —important though these are, but which continue through, and *sometimes in spite of*, all the changes and chances of our imperfect lives'.[1] Because men and women are the imperfect creatures they are, the intention they make at their wedding to stay together cannot itself provide a firm enough foundation for their marriage: it needs to be underpinned by a commitment which is unconditional, which does not depend on feelings, on success or failure, or on any other circumstances. Because it is a commitment to love and to cherish a particular *person* it must necessarily be unconditional. To suggest that the commitment is binding only insofar as the love continues is to attach conditions to the commitment and to ignore the fact that it not only stems from love, but also enables and sustains the love through every kind of circumstance. The love which is in its inception the essence of the commitment may at a later stage, in difficult circumstances, have to be expressed in no more than the sheer determination to hold on—to go on cleaving—though in all other respects love would appear to have fled. For the mutual commitments are acts of will, in which two persons stake themselves and shape their future identities. Though one partner may fail the other in many grievous ways the bond between them remains; it represents not simply a moral obligation to keep their promises, but an 'ontological' reality which has made them what they are.

254. The reasoning from natural theology is supported by reflection on the New Testament witness to the teaching of Jesus. In going behind the Law of Moses to Genesis he was clearly affirming that marriage in the purposes of God is indissoluble. What God *did* in marriage, in creating a 'one flesh' union, was to form a kinship bond analogous to that of blood relationships. Jesus' use of the term 'adultery' to describe the situation of those who divorce their partners and 'remarry' is intelligible only if such a step is not merely disobedient but also in fact impossible. Thus there *can* be no 'remarriage' after divorce.

---

[1] Appendix 3, page 124.

255. Not all of those who believe that the Church's present practice in refusing to remarry is justified accept the full indissolubilist position. For them, while it is clear that Jesus stated that marriage was always intended by God to be an indissoluble relationship, this is not to say that marriages can never be dissolved and new ones contracted. Marriages, in their eyes, *ought not* to be dissolved; they would not, however, go further and say that they *cannot* be dissolved. But this does not affect the position the Church should take if it is to be faithful to the full thrust of Jesus' teaching on marriage. Although the testimony of Mark, Luke and John generally supports the view that Jesus did not see himself as a legislator, it does not follow that what he said has no legislative import or bearing on matters of pastoral discipline. Jesus himself told us that if we love him we are to keep his commandments (John 14. 15), and the Church has always accorded to his words a special authority. The distinction Paul draws between 'Not I but the Lord' and 'I say, not the Lord' (I Cor. 7. 10-12; see paras. 122-3) points to a clear difference between his own authority within the Church and the authority of the Lord of the Church. The commands which Jesus had given his disciples were unquestionable commands for the whole Church. We have to give much careful thought to what they meant and what they should mean for us; nevertheless, the Church must resist attempts to modify their impact or interpret them away. Although the words of Jesus bring fresh insight to each succeeding generation, and scholars can sometimes bring to light points which had escaped the writers of the New Testament, Christianity is the religion of the incarnate Lord, and the testimony of those who stood closest to him in time must have pre-eminent authority.

256. Some Christians accept that Jesus' injunctions were meant literally and apply to them in their individual discipleship, but hesitate to impose them on others as part of the corporate discipline of the Church, for fear of failing in compassion, appearing pharisaical and missing pastoral opportunities. These considerations are important, and should lead the Church to continue the ministry it has exercised, increasingly over the last hundred years, to people whose marriages have ended in breakdown, extending to them, as it does to others who have failed in other respects, the promise of forgiveness and reconciliation. But this does not imply that the Church should compromise its witness to the teaching of its Lord. Institutions are judged less by what they say than by what they do. However much

the Church protested that it still supported the principle of marriage as a life-long union, when people saw it sanctioning remarriage in church, even if only on occasion, they would conclude that the Church had abandoned the teaching of Jesus in face of the secular pressures of the age. If we take Jesus' original prohibition literally we must act on it, not only in our individual discipleship but in our corporate decisions as the Body of Christ.

257. Refusal to remarry need not create a barrier to understanding, nor does it indicate an unforgiving attitude. Undoubtedly Jesus enjoined his followers to be infinitely forgiving; and in responding to the needs of people whose marriages have broken down, as also of those who have failed in other respects, the Church must never say that they are as such outside the fellowship or beyond the reach of Christ's compassion. But it does not follow that the Church should be expected to give its seal of approval to all that they do. Just as parents cannot always altogether approve of what their children do, though they do not condemn them either, so God, although not extreme to mark what is done amiss, must not be supposed to endorse every decision his children make. From this it follows that there should be a certain distancing of the Church from the decisions of an individual member. If his marriage has broken down, and he responsibly and conscientiously decides to enter into a new, legally recognised married relationship, he ought not to expect the Church to perform the ceremony.

258. The case against change represents a reasoned view that the Church's existing discipline is well-founded and, indeed, requires to be reaffirmed with fresh conviction. But the view that the Church should maintain that discipline is reinforced by consideration of the proposals for change. The system by which the bishop or his nominees would decide whether a particular couple could have their marriage solemnised in church would be open to serious objections, and would create as many problems as it solved. In the first place there is a fundamental ambiguity in the concept of a pastoral procedure. The essence of the pastoral approach is that the pastor does not judge but seeks rather to help people to make their own decisions. The attempt to operate the procedure envisaged in a pastoral manner would make it impossible to maintain objective standards and to secure a consistent approach throughout the dioceses. It would soon appear that some dioceses were following a harder and some a softer line, and

the practice of a diocese might well change with a change of bishop. The principle of treating like cases alike could be adhered to only if the Church were to adopt a basically juridical approach, founded on case-law and precedent. This approach, involving searching enquiry, would certainly be cumbersome and expensive: but it would be essential if uniformity of treatment were to be secured. Whichever approach were adopted, there would be a built-in tendency to avoid hard cases and relax standards, leading in the end to indiscriminate remarriage.

259.   The more people seeking to remarry, the more difficult it would prove to operate the diocesan system. The more people permitted to remarry in church, the more open and obvious would be the challenge to the doctrine of marriage as a life-long union.

260.   However the diocesan procedure was operated, it would raise difficulties of principle as well as practice. To distinguish between the sincerely penitent and the others would be a difficult task, and one to be left, according to the Church of England's thinking hitherto, to God alone. It is dubious whether the introduction of a formal process of the kind envisaged with the object of discovering true penitence, would be an acceptable extension of the ministry of the ordained clergy. There would be complaints of unfairness from those whose applications were refused without any reason being given, and—which should be of much greater concern to the Church—from discarded spouses. For example, the wife who had put up with much ill-treatment on the part of her husband because she believed it her Christian duty to do her utmost to salvage her marriage, and who was finally supplanted by another woman, would get a very clear message on what the Church really thought about the sanctity of marriage and how much it really cared for her, if she saw it celebrating their new attachment by a solemn ceremony in church.

261.   Let us suppose for a moment that it did prove possible to operate the procedure pastorally. Even so, unless in practice every request is granted there are going to be some people for whom the Church is pastorally responsible but who are not being allowed remarriage in church. Their position will be much worse than it is at present, since the refusal of remarriage in church will represent a verdict on their own particular case. It will be taken as an outright condemnation, and will create precisely that 'barrier to understanding, and a sense of injustice', leading on occasion to

'permanent alienation from the Church', of which para. 247 speaks. If the Church is to minister to those whose applications are refused, it must maintain a distinction between its ministry of compassion and official permission to remarry in church; yet it is the burden of the argument for remarriage that compassion entails a willingness by the Church in particular cases to remarry.

262. Nor would the proposal achieve the objective stated in para. 248 of ending the existing strain on the conscience of some clergy, and the occasional indiscipline that results. Whereas the present discipline is definite and clear, and intelligible even to those who do not agree with it, the proposed new discipline—unless, again, every request for permission to remarry in church were in fact granted—would give rise to cases where permission was refused for reasons which were not evidently cogent to everyone, and the temptation to act unilaterally would be stronger, not weaker, than it is now, because such action would not be a breach of a universal rule but only a particular judgement. Because the clergyman would remain free in law to remarry divorced persons, the pressure on him to act in a particular case against the diocesan recommendation would increase.

263. If the Church decides to follow the course of action of reaffirming its traditional refusal to marry divorced people, it must in doing so be aware of the risks it may face. The Church can appear to some rigid and uncaring by its refusal to celebrate with people at a major point in their lives. The possibility that this conclusion may be drawn should act as a spur to the Church, and particularly the parish clergy, to develop effective pastoral relationships with those who contract second unions and to indicate the reality of its care for them. Certainly it is possible for a firm refusal to remarry to be seen as a token of the Church's care for a couple, as some evidence received by the Commission indicated. The possibility has also to be faced that a number of clergy will continue to ignore the clear indications of the Church's thinking, even if this were restated in fresh regulations of the General Synod. But the moral force of a considered decision by the Synod to reaffirm the Church's understanding, as the culmination of a decade of careful debate, would be weighty.

264. If on the other hand the Church considers abandoning its traditional rule, it should do so in full awareness of the gravity of the

step. The door once opened could not thereafter be closed: there would be no possibility of a return to the Church's existing marriage discipline. The changes in that discipline which have been proposed are in essence only a variant of the Root proposals which were rejected by the General Synod, and if now adopted would prove deeply divisive of the Church's unity.

(iii) *The case against change reviewed*
265.   It is argued in para. 253 that the commitment of marriage is necessarily unconditional because it is a commitment to love and cherish a particular person, and that the commitment 'enables and sustains the love through every kind of circumstance'. This is indeed true. The commitment which bride and groom make to each other on their wedding day stems from love. It also presumes and wills love. It is unconditional, since it dares to avow the indestructibility of this love whatever may come to pass. Despite the avowal, however, experience shows that love can be destroyed and marriages can break down. Bare cleaving when all hope is gone of a renewal of the marriage relationship is hardly a fulfilment of the original commitment. To assert, when breakdown is complete, that some kind of bond still exists and always will exist is to assert something which can be substantiated neither by the logic of love, nor by the teaching of Jesus, nor by the inspection of actual cases. And when circumstances such as divorce and the remarriage of one of the partners make it impossible for the other partner to hope for reconciliation, the power of the original marriage promise still to bind is, to say the very least, put in question.

266.   Advocates of marriage in church after divorce in exceptional cases acknowledge the force of much of the argument for the Church's existing discipline. A refusal to permit such remarriage seems *prima facie* of a piece both with a life-long commitment and with the words of Jesus. However, to be consistent, a literal interpretation of Jesus' words would involve us in condemning all unions after divorce as adulterous. If that is what Jesus' words mean, individuals have no discretion. Anyone marrying after divorce would be disobeying the Lord, with all the implications that this would involve for Christians in their relations with one another in the Church. The real point of the words of Jesus is a call to everyone with ears to hear to take to heart what marriage is really about. Marriage is for life. There can be no prudential reckoning with the possibility of failure and

breakdown. True love does not, cannot, think in these terms. Nevertheless, failure and breakdown can and do occur. Given the actualities of married life and love, given human weakness and sin, the task facing the Church is to fashion a discipline which holds before those who are married, and those about to marry, the challenge of unconditional love, while offering to those who have failed in their marriage the possibility of a new beginning.

267. The divine forgiveness and command have to be declared to all whose marriages fail: the purpose of the proposed pastoral procedure is to determine whether a couple shows sufficient understanding of both the divine command and the divine forgiveness to justify the Church, for their good and without offence to others, in giving them its blessing. It is already part of the pastoral office of the minister to enquire, gently but firmly, into the spiritual health of those who seek his counsel and aid; what is proposed is a development of, rather than a departure from, Anglican tradition and practice. It must be conceded that there is no way of guaranteeing that in rare cases spiritual hurt may not, unknowingly and unwittingly, be caused to someone who has fought hard to preserve the marriage. No discipline, pastoral or juridical, is infallible. Nevertheless, a careful implementation of the discipline proposed would, by its very discrimination, achieve greater good than the blanket refusal to remarry. There are many today who are spiritually damaged by the Church's present practice.

268. There may be some diversity between diocese and diocese in the way in which pastoral discretion will be exercised, but this does not mean that it will be haphazard. Whatever variation there may be should not be regarded as intolerable, since it will not be a matter of inconsistency over rights and deserts. Someone who is refused remarriage in church may feel 'condemned'. Nevertheless the refusal is made in the best interests of that person. It represents a pastoral judgement that he has not grasped all that such a marriage signifies. It is not a rejection of someone who has disobeyed the teaching of Jesus and can never be forgiven.

269. It is difficult to predict the number of those who would seek remarriage in church, but on present evidence there is no reason to think that the proposed pastoral procedure would be incapable of handling them. The principles underlying the procedure will

discourage the frivolous, encourage the penitent, and increase respect for the Church's witness to the seriousness of marriage.

270. To the charge that a change of discipline would be divisive, it has to be said that the Church is already divided. The dire consequences predicted of the proposed new discipline can with equal force be predicted of the proposal to tighten the existing discipline. The argument that refusal to remarry is essential, if the Church is to maintain a clear witness to life-long marriage, is a recent development, reflecting a deep concern at the increasingly high divorce rate. But the burden of making the witness falls on those who are least well placed to do so, that is, those whose marriages have already broken down. If the previous marriage has already been dissolved there is no positive witness that they can make to its life-long character. Since they experienced no comparable expression of disapproval from the Church at the point where the earlier marriage was being dissolved they are likely to conclude (however illogically) that the Church is not so much opposed to the dissolution of the shell of the earlier marriage as to their attempt to make a reality of marriage in a fresh union. Thus this argument puts the emphasis in the wrong place. In general the refusal by the Church to countenance the possibility of a second marriage out of determination to distance itself from the decisions of individuals, reflects an unwillingness to acknowledge that the contemporary experience of marriage, with all its stresses and uncertainties, may in some respects represent a deeper understanding of what God intends marriage to be. The emphasis on mutuality and sharing, the belief that in marriage each partner can become more fully himself or herself while contributing to the growth of the other—these reflect a certain convergence between secular expectations and Christian understanding which it should be the job of the Church to nourish. In this situation a man or woman who, having experienced failure in that quest, conscientiously seeks in a second marriage a fresh start in the forging of the 'bond of perfectness' deserves to receive all the support the Christian body can offer, including (but not limited to) the celebration of the marriage in church.

OUR CONCLUSIONS RELATING TO REMARRIAGE IN CHURCH
271. We have not been able to come to a common mind in regard to remarriage in church. As will have become apparent, we all take a

'high' view of marriage. The life-long commitment of a man and a woman to each other is a necessary prerequisite if the relationship is legally to be one of marriage: it is also the foundation upon which may be built the house of love in which husband and wife together dwell. But the majority of us consider that the best witness to that view of marriage will be offered by a pastoral ministry which includes, in particular circumstances, the marriage of some divorced persons in church. We believe that the Church of England ought now to be prepared, in appropriate cases and on the basis of a diocesan decision, to allow this. A minority of us consider that the Church should continue to refuse to marry divorced people, believing that to depart now from a long held position would compromise the Church in its witness to the society in which we live. One among us taking this view regards marriage as indissoluble. Others of us see no theological objection to second marriages but powerful practical objections to allowing such marriages to take place in church.

272. We set out in summary form below the two courses of action open to the Church, indicating the degree of support each has received within the Commission, and trust that the General Synod will be assisted thereby in coming to its own decision.

Course A

(1) The Church of England should now take steps to revise its regulations to permit a divorced person, with the permission of the bishop, to be married in church during the lifetime of a former spouse.

(2) The marriage of divorced persons in church should be solemnised by the use of one or other of the existing permitted orders for the solemnisation of marriage, with the addition of an appropriate invariable Preface.

(3) The working of the new procedure should be reviewed after a specified period of years.[1]

Course B

The Church of England should restate by Act of Synod its belief that, in order to maintain its witness to the principle of life-long obligation which is inherent in every legally contracted marriage, the Church should not allow the use of the marriage service in the case of anyone who has a former partner still living.[2]

---

[1]The members of the Commission who support this course of action are as follows: the Bishop of Lichfield; the Ven. M. E. Adie; Mrs S. Aglionby; Mrs M. I. Allen; Canon Prof. J. Atkinson: Canon Prof. P. R. Baelz (Consultant); Chancellor T. A. C. Coningsby; Mrs J. Dann; the Very Rev. B. D. Jackson; Prof. Kathleen Jones; Canon Barnabas Lindars, SSF; Dr K. Soddy; Dr H. Morgan Williams.

[2]The members of the Commission who support this course of action are as follows: Chancellor Sheila Cameron; Mrs M. E. R. Holmes; Mr J. R. Lucas; the Rev. M. Whittock.

273. *We accordingly recommend by a majority that Course A be adopted.*

274. After we had begun to meet as a Commission two matters were referred to us for our consideration which, while related to our main task, were sufficiently distinct from it to merit separate treatment. These relate to the marriage in church of people who have not been baptised, and the legal position of ordinands or clergymen who are divorced or have married divorced persons. We report on each of these matters below.

MARRIAGE OF THE UNBAPTISED

275. When the Archbishops' Commission on Canon Law reported in 1947, a draft Canon was included relating to the marriage in church of the unbaptised. In the introduction it was stated that the Canon 'forbids any minister to allow his church to be used for a marriage where both the parties are unbaptised, and in the case of two persons desiring to be married in his church, of which one is not baptised, the Canon orders the minister to refer the matter to the bishop and to obey therein his order and direction'.[1]

276. By 1959 the relevant clause of the Canon had been approved by both Convocations and by the House of Laity in the following form:

2. No minister shall solemnise matrimony, or allow matrimony to be solemnised in the church or chapel of which he is the minister, between two persons neither of whom has been baptised; and if two persons, one of whom has not been baptised, desire to be so married, he shall refer the matter to the bishop of the diocese and obey therein his order and direction.

277. In the accompanying Report by the Canon Law Steering Committee of the Convocations the following note was appended:

Clause 2 of this Canon is not in accordance with the law and legislation will be necessary. If parties are entitled to be married by residence in the parish, etc., a minister has no power at present to refuse because neither of the parties is baptised. As any legislation will amend the marriage law and affect civil rights it may be thought that legislation in this case should be by Parliamentary Bill rather than by Church Assembly Measure.

278. In the event no legislation was promoted and therefore, when the Canon came to be promulged,[2] paragraph 2 was omitted as being repugnant to the statute law. It was hoped that the paragraph could

---

[1]*The Canon Law of the Church of England* (SPCK, 1947), p. 126.
[2]Now Canon B30 (*Of Holy Matrimony*).

be included when enabling legislation was subsequently passed.

279. The Archbishops' Commission on Church and State (the Chadwick Commission) considered the matter. In their report *Church and State*, published in 1970, they suggested that the solemnisation of such marriages should be at the discretion of the parish priest, guided by such regulations as might be made from time to time by the General Synod. The Commission considered that the clergyman should not be compelled by law to solemnise such a marriage, but that equally he should not be prevented by law from doing so, if he considered it warranted by the pastoral needs of the situation in a particular case.[1]

280. In 1975 the House of Bishops accepted a common policy with regard to marriage by common licence as opposed to marriage by banns. It was agreed that a licence should not issue where neither party is baptised, and, where only one party is baptised, it should be stated in the application form that the other party does not reject the Christian faith and desires marriage in church. The House felt able to make this rule because a common licence is a privilege granted by the Church and not a right of the parties.

281. The Legal Advisory Commission of the General Synod have considered this subject on a number of occasions and have confirmed the view that, as the law stands at present, baptism is not an essential qualification for the solemnisation of marriage in church, and that the clergy are not entitled to refuse to marry such persons after due publication of banns. The Advisory Commission consider that a reform along the lines suggested by the Chadwick Commission should be implemented without delay.

282. As we have recognised elsewhere in this report, marriage in church provides the clergy with a valuable pastoral opportunity to commend the riches of the Christian understanding of marriage to many who would not otherwise encounter it. In that sense it represents one of many occasions for the preaching of the Gospel. We believe occasions such as these are appreciated by the clergy, even though they may not necessarily lead to a decision by an unbaptised person to ask for baptism. On the other hand we consider it is objectionable for a clergyman to be required to marry a couple, one or

---

[1]*Op. cit.*, pp. 61-2.

both of whom not only refuse baptism but explicitly reject the Christian faith.

283. We share the view of the Chadwick Commission that the pastoral judgement of the clergyman concerned in any particular case is likely in general to produce the best solution. *We therefore recommend that legislation be introduced to remove the present obligation on the clergy to marry unbaptised people, and that the solemnisation of such marriages should be at the discretion of the minister subject to the advice of the Bishop.*

THE MARRIAGE AND DIVORCE OF ORDINANDS AND CLERGYMEN

284. Earlier in this chapter we referred to the problems created when married clergymen faced stress in their marriages. In an increasing number of cases the breakdown of marriage is being followed by divorce and remarriage. The increasing number of people who have been divorced is also leading to a growing number of ordinands and clergymen themselves marrying, or seeking to marry, divorced women.

285. We have acknowledged the importance of dealing with the marriage difficulties of the clergy in an understanding and pastoral manner. Divorce and remarriage among the clergy however create an added problem for the Church since they touch on matters of clergy discipline, which is largely (though not entirely) governed by the terms of statute law and Canons. Part of the problem is created by the changing social circumstances in which the Church carries on its ministry, part by the circumstance that the Church of England, as the established Church, may not legislate to regulate its own affairs in ways repugnant to the law of the land.

286. In the next three sections we describe the character of the Church's law and practice relating to the marriage and divorce of ordinands and clergy. We then consider the significance of these in the light of our general approach to marriage and divorce, and conclude by recommending changes which we believe will meet some of the difficulties facing the Church in regard to this matter.[1]

---

[1] In what we say concerning the application of the law we have been greatly benefited in forming our own judgements by the advice of Sir Harold Kent, QC, GCB, at the time Dean of the Arches.

287. The practice of the Church of England in admitting men to ordination is governed by Canon C.4. Paragraph 1 of this Canon requires the bishop to be satisfied that an ordinand is 'of virtuous conversation and good repute and such as to be a wholesome example and pattern to the flock of Christ'. These words would justify the bishop in refusing ordination to an ordinand who had been divorced by his wife on the ground that the breakdown of the marriage was due to his adultery, desertion or behaviour making it unreasonable for her to live with him. Divorce in these circumstances would make an ordained clergyman liable to deprivation under the Ecclesiastical Jurisdiction Measure 1963, as amended; although there is no comparable provision for ordinands it is inconceivable that conduct which justified deprivation would not be a ground for refusing ordination.

288. On the other hand an ordinand whose marriage had been dissolved otherwise than through his fault could not be brought within the terms of paragraph 1 of Canon C.4. As such he could not be refused ordination on the simple ground of divorce, though it might be said that he had failed to make his marriage into a permanent and life-long union and in this respect would not be an example and pattern to his flock.

289. There is clearly room for differences of judgement here, especially with increasing awareness of the complexities of the marriage relationship and the difficulties of ascribing blame for breakdown. Where however an ordinand remarries or marries a divorced woman, paragraph 3 of Canon C.4 is unambiguous:

> 3. No person shall be admitted into Holy Orders who has remarried and, the wife of that marriage being alive, has a former wife still living; or who is married to a person who has been previously married and whose former husband is still living.

This was a new canonical provision introduced in the 1969 code, and was authorised by the nearly identical section 9 of the Clergy (Ordination and Miscellaneous Provisions) Measure 1964. The effect is clear. It imposes an absolute ban on the ordination of a man who has remarried during the lifetime of his former wife. And it equally refuses ordination to a man if he is married to a divorced woman during the lifetime of her former husband.

Institution of Clergy to Benefices

290.   As we have already seen (para. 287) a clergyman is liable to be deprived of his benefice if a divorce is granted against him on a finding of his adultery, desertion or intolerable conduct. *A fortiori* it would be a bar to his institution to a benefice. A divorce in itself, without such a finding, would not appear to be a ground for disciplinary proceedings, and a clergyman could therefore be instituted to a benefice.

291.   If however the clergyman subsequently remarries during the lifetime of his former spouse the position becomes less clear. The only relevant grounds on which the bishop may refuse to institute are set out in Canon C.10, paragraph 3(b); they are that '. . . the said priest is unfit for the discharge of the duties of a benefice by reason of . . . grave misconduct or neglect of duty in an ecclesiastical office, evil life, having by his conduct caused grave scandal concerning his moral character since his ordination . . .'.

292.   These words do not seem to us apt to cover remarriage during the lifetime of a former spouse, which is an act allowed by the secular law and countenanced by society in general, and not carrying the moral imputations of such words as 'grave misconduct', 'evil life' and 'grave scandal'.

293.   That, however, is not the end of the matter. The words quoted above from Canon C.10 are a verbatim reproduction of words contained in section 2(1)(b) of the Benefices Act 1898, and that Act makes it clear (which the Canon does not) that the grounds set out in the section are not exhaustive. Obviously they do not cover grounds of doctrine or ritual, but they also do not necessarily cover all grounds of 'conduct'. There is authority for the proposition that conduct constituting an ecclesiastical offence (which is defined in section 14(1) of the Ecclesiastical Jurisdiction Measure 1963 as including 'conduct unbecoming the office and work of a Clerk in Holy Orders' and also includes any breach of Canon law), is a ground for refusing institution.

294.   The phrase 'conduct unbecoming the office and work of a clergyman' has a strong suggestion of immoral or scandalous conduct, and would not naturally cover lawful remarriage, which may be undertaken with great seriousness and responsibility, even though it undoubtedly follows upon a failure to live up to the Christian

understanding of marriage. Nor do the Canons provide any support for the attempt to found an ecclesiastical offence upon the fact of remarriage. The only relevant Canons are Canon B.30, paragraph 1, which sets out the Church's doctrine of marriage as a permanent and life-long union,[1] paragraph 3 of the same Canon, which requires the minister to explain that doctrine to the intending parties to a marriage in church, and Canon C.26, paragraph 2, which requires a minister 'to frame and fashion his life and that of his family according to the doctrine of Christ, and to make himself and them, so far as in him lies, wholesome examples and patterns to the flock of Christ'. Though Canon C.26 points to the standard expected of clergy, the saving words 'so far as in him lies' would make it difficult to regard marriage breakdown, whether or not followed by remarriage, as the kind of breach which should be treated as an ecclesiastical offence.

295.   Another factor is that under section 3 of the Benefices Act 1898 an appeal lies from a refusal to institute on any non-doctrinal ground, not only the grounds set out in section 2 of the Act. The appeal is heard by a Court consisting of the Archbishop of the Province and a Judge of the Supreme Court. It is for the Judge to decide all questions of law and fact and his findings are binding on the Archbishop, who then decides whether institution should be granted or refused. It would therefore be for the Judge to decide whether the remarriage constituted a valid ground for refusal, either as falling within the language of section 2 of the Act or as constituting an ecclesiastical offence. In view of recent changes in the divorce law it would be difficult for him to make such a finding. The sole ground for a divorce is now the irretrievable breakdown of the marriage. If remarriage in these circumstances is to be regarded as a ground for disqualification for preferment, a Judge might well take the view that the Church ought to say so (as in the case of ordination) in unmistakable terms.

296.   There is no reported case of an appeal under this procedure against refusal to institute. If a bishop thought it right to refuse to institute on the ground that the clergyman's remarriage made it difficult for him to teach the Church's doctrine on marriage effectively and to set a good example to his parishioners in this respect as required by the Canons, he might well escape challenge in the Court. On the other hand the Act requires the bishop to specify the grounds

---

[1]See para. 152 above.

of his refusal to the patron and the clergyman to be instituted, so the possibility of the matter being taken to the Court sooner or later is a real one.

Proceedings against beneficed clergymen
297. The question also arises whether disciplinary proceedings can be brought against a beneficed clergyman on the grounds of his divorce and remarriage. Proceedings are in the main governed by the provisions of the Ecclesiastical Jurisdiction Measure 1963. This provides for the proceedings to come before the ecclesiastical courts, rather than the Judge of the Supreme Court appointed under the Benefices Act 1898.

298. A clergyman can undoubtedly be proceeded against on the ground that a divorce had been granted against him on a finding of his adultery, desertion or intolerable conduct; if the facts were established he would be liable, as we have seen, to deprivation. Common to this and to other types of behaviour which provide the grounds for disciplinary proceedings is the element of immoral or scandalous conduct. 'Conduct unbecoming the office and work of a Clerk in Holy Orders' is to be interpreted in these terms and would not, therefore, be held to cover a case of divorce and remarriage unaccompanied by scandal or misconduct.

Recommendations
299. It is clear that the law on the marriage and divorce of ordinands and clergy is confusing and, in some respects, doubtful. A bishop may find his ability to deal pastorally with a particular case is limited by the terms of Statute or Canon; conversely a situation may arise where there is a clear need in the interests of the Church to take action which however is ruled out by the present provisions of the law.

300. A majority of us consider that remarriage following divorce or marriage to a divorced woman should not be automatically regarded as conduct inconsistent with the standard required by the Church of ordinands. We believe that the best course in these difficult circumstances is for the bishop to have a complete discretion. *We therefore by a majority recommend legislation which will give the diocesan bishop discretion whether or not to ordain a man who (a) having been divorced has remarried during the lifetime of his former wife; or (b) has married a divorced woman during the lifetime of her former husband.*

301. We are however all agreed that there may be circumstances where a bishop might judge that it would not be right to institute a divorced and remarried clergyman or one who marries a divorced woman. Under the existing law the bishop's power to refuse to institute in such a situation is not assured. Here again, though for a different reason, it seems best to proceed by way of a discretionary power. *We therefore recommend legislation which will give the diocesan bishop discretion whether or not to institute a clergyman who (a) having been divorced has remarried during the lifetime of his former wife; or (b) has married a divorced woman during the lifetime of her former husband.*

302. Where a beneficed clergyman is divorced, whether or not he subsequently remarries, the primary consideration should be the consequences for his continued ability to carry out the office and work of a priest. If scandal or clear misconduct is established the provisions of section 14(1) of the Ecclesiastical Jurisdiction Measure appear to us to be appropriate. Otherwise, the criterion to be employed should be the likelihood of pastoral breakdown. We consider that in these circumstances the situation is best handled under the provisions of the Incumbents (Vacation of Benefices) Measure.

CONCLUSION
303. Marriage is about a man and a woman setting out soberly and joyfully to build a life for themselves. Married life provides the setting for the deepest and most fundamental human experience that most people will have; and, despite the failures, we can be encouraged by the high seriousness with which most people approach this most crucial of personal relationships. The Church has a responsibility to witness to the importance of marriage and family life, to help young couples through the difficult and often harassing tasks of founding a family in what is in many ways a hostile environment; but it also has a responsibility to show compassion and understanding towards those whose marriages fail and to help them to find new means of personal stability and social trust.

304. We have indicated some of the reasons why the irretrievable breakdown of marriage may occur more frequently than in the past. We have discussed both new and increasing sources of stress in contemporary married life, stress that may threaten and cause failure in personal relationships long before a marriage is past mending and the parties resort to a divorce court. Our pastoral care requires the

best of our spiritual resources, together with sociological and psychological understanding, in order that we may be sensitive in our concern for the dilemmas and the welfare of individuals. As the Joint Committee of the Convocations of Canterbury and York concluded in their report of 1971, 'In dealing with human tragedies and failures, no solution worth the name can be tidy and simple'. We trust that our analysis of the courses of action open to the Church will enable it to meet the demands of its ministry in a way which is both sensitive to the needs of persons and faithful to the insight into marriage it has received from God.

Summary of the Recommendations of the Marriage Commission

1. We recommend that the Convocation regulations requiring that those who marry after divorce should only be admitted to Communion with the permission of the Bishop should be rescinded.
(Page 77)

2. We recommend that the present use of services of prayer and dedication in connection with remarriage after divorce should be brought to an end. (Page 84)

3. We recommend—*by majority*—that:

(1) The Church of England should now take steps to revise its regulations to permit a divorced person with the permission of the bishop to be married in church during the lifetime of a former spouse.

(2) The marriage of divorced persons in church should be solemnised by the use of one or other of the existing permitted orders for the solemnisation of marriage, with the addition of an appropriate invariable Preface.

(3) The working of the new procedure should be reviewed after a specified period of years. (Page 100)

4. We recommend that legislation be introduced to remove the present obligation on the clergy to marry unbaptised people, and that the solemnisation of such marriages should be at the discretion of the minister subject to the advice of the Bishop. (Page 103)

5. We recommend—*by majority*—legislation which will give the diocesan bishop discretion whether or not to ordain a man who:

(a) having been divorced has remarried during the lifetime of his former wife; or

(b) has married a divorced woman during the lifetime of her former husband. (Page 107)

6. We recommend legislation which will give the diocesan bishop discretion whether or not to institute a clergyman who:

(a) having been divorced has remarried during the lifetime of his former wife; or

(b) has married a divorced woman during the lifetime of her former husband. (Page 108)

1

Marriage and Divorce Statistics

TABLE I MARRIAGES 1961-75 (thousands, England and Wales)

	All marriages	First marriages	
		Men	Women
1961	346.7	308.8	312.3
1966	384.5	339.1	342.7
1970	415.5	361.1	364.4
1971	404.7	343.6	347.4
1972	426.2	343.3	348.0
1973	400.4	318.6	321.1
1974	384.4	302.3	304.6
1975	380.6	296.0	298.2

Source: Population Trends 7, Office of Population Censuses and Surveys, Spring 1977, Table 23.

TABLE II DIVORCES 1961-75 (thousands, England and Wales)

	Petitions filed	Decrees made absolute
1961	31.9	25.4
1966	46.6	39.1
1970	71.7	58.2
1971	110.9	74.4
1972	110.7	119.0
1973	115.5	106.0
1974	131.7	113.5
1975	140.1	120.5

Source: Population Trends, 7, OPCS, Table 24.

TABLE III REMARRIAGE OF THE DIVORCED, 1961-75
(thousands, England and Wales)

	Men	Women
1961	18.8	18.0
1966	26.7	25.1
1970	35.7	33.7
1971	42.4	39.6
1972	63.0	58.1
1973	62.4	59.6
1974	64.1	61.7
1975	67.0	64.7

Source: Population Trends, 7, OPCS, Table 23.

TABLE IV   NUMBER OF CHILDREN INVOLVED IN DISSOLUTIONS
AND ANNULMENTS OF MARRIAGE, 1972 (England and Wales)

Couples with		Numbers of children involved
No children	30,824	Nil
One child	29,538	29,538
Two children	31,392	62,784
Three children	15,235	45,705
Four children	6,817	27,268
Five or more children	5,219	30,384
		195,679

Notes

(i) numbers of children refer to surviving children at the time of divorce, and include adopted children and children legitimised by marriage.

(ii) 131,112 of these children were under the age of 16 at the time of the divorce, and 30,261 under the age of five. OPCS now only counts as 'children' of divorcing couples those under the age of 16. The number of these in 1975 was 145,096, 33,372 being under the age of five. (OPCS Monitor, 7 March 1977).

Source: Registrar General's Annual Review of the Population, 1974. OPCS information.

TABLE V   TEENAGE MARRIAGES (England and Wales)

	Men		Women	
	Numbers aged 16-19 at marriage (thousands)	*Per cent bachelors marrying under the age of 20*	*Numbers aged 16-19 at marriage (thousands)*	*Per cent spinsters marrying under the age of 20*
1961	16.6	6.9	77.0	28.7
1966	22.1	9.9	82.7	32.5
1970	27.2	10.1	95.4	30.8
1971	26.0	10.1	93.5	31.1
1972	26.0	10.2	93.6	31.3
1973	24.7	10.6	88.2	32.2
1974	22.9	10.5	81.0	32.2
1975	20.9	10.1	75.8	31.7

Source: Population Trends, 7, OPCS, Table 23.

TABLE VI   DIVORCE UNDER THE AGE OF 25
(thousands, England and Wales)

	Men	Women
1961	1.4	2.4
1966	2.6	4.1
1970	4.4	6.7
1971	4.9	7.5
1972	8.2	11.7
1973	8.7	11.8
1974	10.3	11.4
1975	12.1	13.0

Source: Population Trends, 7, OPCS, Table 24.

TABLE VII   MARRIAGE BY MANNER OF SOLEMNISATION, 1964, 1970
and 1975 (per cent of all marriages in a given year, England and Wales)

A—*All marriages*

	Anglican	Other religious ceremony	Civil
1964	46.7	22.4	30.9
1970	41.0	19.5	39.5
1975	34.9	17.3	47.8

B—*First marriage*

	Anglican	Other religious ceremony	Civil
1964	53.8	24.2	22.0
1970	48.6	21.2	30.2
1975	48.6	19.5	31.9

C—*Remarriage of divorced persons*

	Anglican	Other religious ceremony	Civil
1964	—	11.3	88.7
1970	0.2	10.8	89.0
1975	0.5	11.4	88.2

Source: OPCS information.

Notes

(i)   Table VIIC refers to marriages in which one party or both were divorced.

(ii) The actual number of such marriages by Anglican ceremony was:

1964	62
1970	127
1975	476

TABLE VIII   NUMBER OF MARRIAGES IN 1975 WHERE ONE OR BOTH
PARTIES WAS DIVORCED, BY MANNER OF SOLEMNISATION

	One party divorced	*Both parties divorced*
Anglican	411	65
Roman Catholic	666	32
Free Church	8,792	1,668
Civil ceremony	57,800	30,118
Total	67,669	31,883

Source: OPCS information.

2
Nullity and the Roman Catholic Church

1. The Report has referred to the question of nullity and the extension of its use by the Roman Catholic Church in the consideration of the courses of action open to the Church of England in reviewing its present discipline concerning the marriage of divorced persons, and in the treatment of the development in attitude of the law to marriage and divorce. For its part, the Roman Catholic Church in the United Kingdom will only consider a request for a decree of nullity once the marriage has been dissolved in the civil court. It must be added however that the same relationship between civil and ecclesiastical jurisdiction is not reflected in many other countries and, for example, in Spain the Roman Catholic Church is the only authority which can dissolve marriages. The purpose of this appendix is to draw out, as a brief guide, the main grounds of nullity now accepted by the Roman Catholic Church and the procedure by which annulments to marriages may be granted.

2. The main impediments (or grounds for nullity) are those which in one way or another militate against the very tenet of the Catholic understanding of Christian marriage. The Pastoral Constitution of the Second Vatican Council, *The Church in the Modern World*, summarises the three main pillars of Christian marriage thus, 'A man and a woman who, by the marriage covenant of conjugal love "are no longer two, but one flesh", render mutual help and service to each other through an intimate union of their persons and of their actions . . . As a mutual gift of two persons, this intimate union, as well as the good of the children, imposes total fidelity on the spouses and argues for an unbreakable bond between them'. These three basic elements are thus permanence, exclusiveness and, arising from this union, the possibility of procreation. Any factor which denies any one of these three elements of the union can be made a ground for nullity and is referred to as 'partial simulation'. They are described under the following heads:

(i) *An intention against children*
A positive and deliberate intention on the part of one partner to

withhold from the other true marital rights. Such an intention must be shown to be a deliberate act of will by one of the partners. It might also be added that there would be no grounds for nullity where there was a *mutual* decision not to procreate.

(ii) *An intention against indissolubility*
A positive and deliberate intention on the part of one partner against the indissolubility of the marriage bond. Marriage by its nature is a commitment to a permanent and indissoluble union. A partner who as a deliberate act of will regards it as anything less may provide grounds for a decree of nullity.

(iii) *An intention against fidelity*
A positive and deliberate intention on the part of one partner to exclude from the marriage consent the obligation of fidelity to the other partner.

An annulment on the grounds of *total simulation* is more rare but not unknown. In this situation it would have to be proven that one of the partners, who to all external appearances had given consent to the marriage, nonetheless had no clear firm intention within him or herself to make such a contract. There are strict rules regarding the admissibility of evidence in such cases.

3. The other main grounds for nullity are as follows:

(i) *Force and Fear*
The marriage consent was given under coercion of such a kind that one of the partners was placed in such a state of grave fear from which the only escape was to enter the marriage. Such force and fear must always come from an external factor and be sufficient to interfere with a person's liberty of consent.

(ii) *Amentia*
Each person must be able freely to exercise his will in consenting to the marriage. Any condition (usually some form of severe mental disorder) which resulted in either partner being in a position where he or she was unable to bring their mind to bear to such a consent would constitute, after careful scrutiny, grounds for nullity.

(iii) *Ignorance of the nature of marriage*
One of the partners was totally ignorant of the true nature of marriage. A high level of knowledge is not required of a couple but

they must have grasped the basic tenet of the permanence of the union and the possibility (and practicalities) of procreation arising from it.

The Roman Catholic Church has recently made a significant extension of admissible grounds for nullity. These new grounds are set out in the following heads.

(iv) *Lack of due discretion*

Both couples who desire to enter into a marriage contract must be able fully to appreciate and understand the implications of marriage. The notion of due discretion recognises that in some cases one partner may, through reasons of individual and psychological immaturity, be unable to make an acceptable consent to a marriage contract. There has been a significant increase in the number of petitions for decrees of nullity on these grounds. The decision rests with the judges of the tribunal who ascertain whether an individual had significant 'maturity' at the time of his or her marriage fully to comprehend the obligations which marriage laid upon them. The judgement rests solely on an evaluation of an individual's appreciation of the concept of marriage at the time of the wedding. It is very different from the ground of amentia in the sense that the judgement would demonstrate that one of the partners though possibly highly articulate and intelligent nevertheless lacked 'due discretion' with regard to marriage and its obligations.

(v) *Inability to fulfil the obligations of marriage*

Such a ground for nullity is proven after the marriage has been contracted. An example would be the continued adultery by one partner with third parties.

(vi) *Error*

There are two grounds of error under this heading. One is the more obvious ground where there has been mistaken identity. The other is more complex and involves the quality of the person involved i.e. where on account of the emergence of new facts subsequent to the marriage a qualitative change in a partner is regarded as having taken place. Such an error of quality has been described thus: 'where the quality of the person (concerning which there is error) is so significant and substantial as to make him (or her) a different person without such a quality'. (Ralph Brown, *Marriage Annulment in the Catholic Church*, p. 43.)

4. Some other grounds for nullity also require the submission of oral evidence. These describe cases where a boy or girl has married before the ages of 16 and 14 respectively. This hardly applies in England and Wales where the civil law stipulates that no marriages may be contracted in which either party is below 16 years of age. An impediment would also exist in cases of abduction or where one partner has conspired with a third party to murder the other. Impediments also arise out of certain family relationships. For example, it is forbidden for a parent to marry an adopted child (this accords with the civil law) or for a person to marry the immediate relations of the partner with whom he or she is living, but not technically married to because of an impediment.

5. Another major ground for a decree of nullity is that of impotence on the part of one partner (i.e. where a partner by reason of an antecedent and perpetual condition was incapable of performing the marriage act). An impediment to a marriage also exists where a partner places conditions upon a marriage which are not verified.

6. Some impediments however do not require such oral evidence and can be dealt with administratively as documents can usually verify the position. Examples of this are where a partner is still bound by a contract of marriage, or where the necessary form of marriage was not observed. There are also the impediments of consanguinity and affinity. An impediment to marriage also exists for those who have taken Holy Orders or who have taken solemn vows (i.e. to a religious order).

7. We have thus far described the main grounds of nullity. Set out below, in brief form, is the outline of the procedure which is followed prior to the granting (if the tribunal so finds) of a decree of nullity.

(a) *Initial application*
Interview with the prospective petitioner may be conducted by an advocate (a person who assists a petitioner to prepare his case) or by one of the number of judges who assist the tribunal.
It is the task of the president of the tribunal to ensure that a competent service of interviewing is available for prospective petitioners.
After the interview and where it seems likely that a case could be made for the dissolution of a marriage on the grounds of a particular impediment(s), the interviewing priest will assist the petitioner in

drawing up a statement of his case or, as it is called, the Libellus. It may be added that a significant number of cases do not get beyond initial applications as it may be considered that there are insufficient grounds for nullity.

(b) *Formal Petition*
Elements in the Petition.

(1) Names, address, religion, dates of birth, date and place of marriage.

(2) State competence i.e. grounds for the court's legal ability to accept and try the case as opposed to the right of some other tribunal to do so.

(3) Alleged ground(s) of nullity.

(4) Alleged facts indicating *prima facie* case (pre- and post-marriage history).

(5) Accompanying documents:
　(a) Certificates of baptism and marriage
　(b) Nomination of advocate
　(c) List of witnesses
　(d) Medical reports—if applicable.

(c) *Presentation of Petition*
Constitution of tribunal.

(1) President.

(2) Defender of the bond of marriage (a priest skilled in Canon Law, whose role it is to look after the interests of the bond of marriage).

(3) Advocate.

(4) Notary (a priest who takes down the testimony at formal evidence sessions and whose signature on the documents shows that they and other papers in the case are authentic).

The case is then either formally rejected (reasons would be stated) or given formal acceptance. At this point the Ponens (who can also be the President) is appointed. This person leads the discussion of the case at the decision hearing and eventually produces what is known as the 'sentence' which sets out in law and fact the reasons for the decision of the tribunal.

The respondent is then informed of the ensuing proceedings in a citation which gives details of the case before the court, the date of its first meeting, and inviting evidence. The respondent can then reply stating whether he or she wishes to give evidence or leave the matter in the hands of the court.

(d) *Contestatio Litis*

At this stage the tribunal agrees the precise grounds of the alleged nullity. A document is then prepared setting out the grounds, the names of the members of the Court (the petitioner may object to any name) and the citation of the respondent and the reply if any. The document is signed by the judges, defender, advocate and the notary. The evidence of the petitioner may also be heard at this point.

(e) *Formal Hearing: Evidence*

Petitioner and any witnesses give evidence.

When individual testimony is completed the whole deposition is read back to the witness. It should be added that the deposition is not a verbatim account and it may be altered at this stage by a witness.

All those present then sign the document.

Where witnesses are in distant places a request is sent to that diocese which arranges for testimony to be given.

This testimony is then passed to the court.

(f) *Final Procedures*

Once the formal process of receiving evidence is completed and the advocate and defender of the bond are satisfied, the evidence is 'published', and is then studied by the advocate and defender of the bond who may decide to hear more evidence.

From the evidence the advocate shows why the marriage may be declared null and void. These statements are then passed to the defender of the bond who in his turn uses the evidence to show why the marriage should remain valid.

(g) *Decision*

All the evidence and comments by the advocate and defender are submitted to the judges for consideration. After the Ponens has submitted his statement the decision is then taken (on the basis of a majority view) whether or not there are sufficient grounds for nullity. The petitioner, the advocate and the defender are informed of the decision. The Ponens then draws up the sentence (see para. 7(c)).

(h) *Appeal*
Right of Appeal by the petitioner.
An Appeal, on the basis of the present law, must be made by the defender of the bond if the judges decide in favour of granting a decree of nullity.

(i) *Decision at second instance*
If at Appeal stage the court has found that it appears proven that a marriage is null and void the defender must prepare a short report on the case for consideration of a court of second instance. Where the defender does not feel there are any special problems the appeal court will proceed to ratify the decision of the court of first instance (ratification).

If, however, there appear to be special problems the 'ordinary procedure' is adopted and the defender and advocate submit further comments and the case is reconsidered by judges with their decision fully explained by the Ponens.

If this second instance decision accords with the first instance decision a decree of nullity will be granted. Where a petitioner receives an affirmative and negative decision the case is referred to the Sacred Roman Rota (this third hearing can take place on the local diocesan level) for a third hearing. If, at this stage, there is an affirmative decision a decree of nullity may be granted. In some circumstances a petitioner (following a negative decision) may appeal after the first stage to the Rota. In such cases where there was an affirmative decision by the Rota it would necessitate a third hearing by the Rota (with a different panel of judges) to confirm the decision one way or another.

3
Indissolubility

The word 'indissolubility' is used in several senses, and there are many varying arguments for and against the indissolubility of marriage. Sometimes marriages are said to be indissoluble in the sense that they *ought not* to be dissolved, more usually (and in this Appendix) in the sense that they *cannot* be dissolved. Sometimes what is referred to is the whole complex of social, personal, moral and spiritual realities that go to make up a marriage, sometimes only the social, only the personal, or only the moral and spiritual. It is difficult to disentangle these, because in a happy marriage they go together. Thus our concept of marriage is formed by the many instances in which the ideal is realised and in which 'is' and 'ought' coincide. In the un-ideal cases, in which marriages break down, it is difficult to determine the relative importance of the different strands which combine to constitute the marriage bond and the cogency of the arguments for and against its indissolubility. Sometimes it seems a mere verbal quibble whether or not a regular relationship entered into by someone who has been divorced should be described as a marriage. But words are important as expressing what we have in mind. Hence we have to be clear what is and what is not essential to the Christian understanding of marriage.

It is clear that, empirically speaking, marriages can be dissolved. Couples can part company and go their separate ways. Even when they do not separate, the marriage may from a personal point of view be dead, each person meaning nothing to the other, although continuing to live under the same roof. It is also generally admitted that in some circumstances, although regrettable, it may be best for a couple to separate. In such a case it is being accepted that the social relationship that constitutes marriage ought to be dissolved. Where a marriage has in this empirical sense been dissolved, it is possible, although not always countenanced by law or public opinion, for the parties to form new relationships with others which satisfy the empirical criteria for marriage. People can live together, and may remain together for life. That this can happen is not in dispute. The question for the Christian, however, is whether these empirical facts are the determinative features of marriage, or whether there are in addition moral and spiritual factors which have their own validity; and, if there are, whether they can be nullified by the partners or terminated by formal process.

The indissolubilist tradition in the Church maintains that marriage involves a moral commitment and a spiritual bond which are not merely a function of the empirical manifestations of marriage—shared home, sexual relationship, children, etc.—important though these are, but which continue through, and *sometimes in spite of*, all the changes and chances of our imperfect lives. Marriage is not merely a living together that happens, but a life-long union of wills as well as of bodies, and is constituted not merely by intentions, which can change, but by promises, which cannot. This tradition is based partly on a natural theology of marriage, partly on the Church's understanding of the teaching of Jesus, and sometimes on a reading of Ephesians 5.

What marriage is can best be understood by comparing it with what it is not. Besides casual relationships between men and women, there are many that are relatively stable. Some are intended to be 'trial marriage'. They are childless and, if things do not work out, can be dissolved without breach of faith; but if they prove satisfactory they are usually regularised in due course. Other couples do not get married, not because they are not yet sure, but because they want always to feel unfettered. They have children, and fully intend to live together for the duration of their lives; but they have conscientious objections against the institution of marriage, and often maintain that their association is more genuine and authentic because it depends all the time for its continuance on their continuing to wish it to continue. Other couples enter into a commitment which is public but not necessarily permanent: thus some 'Hollywood marriages' are formal legal arrangements which alter the legal rights and duties of the respective parties as long as the marriage lasts, but can be ended either by consent or, in some cases, unilaterally. Both parties recognise this possibility from the outset. Other unions are intended to be permanent, but not guaranteed to be. Such would be the case with civil marriage under a jurisdiction which makes it an explicit condition of marriage that the parties should intend to enter life-long union, but which does not hold them bound by their former intentions if subsequently they change their minds. In other cases there may be guarantees, but not cast-iron ones: the parties would not only express their intentions, but they would also make their promises, which will bind them provided the going does not get *too* rough— 'I take thee for better, for worse (within reasonable limits)'.

All these kinds of union are possible. The Church has, perhaps, in time past been too undiscriminating in its condemnation of unions which fall short of the Christian ideal of marriage. Rather than denounce all the parties concerned as 'living in sin', we should be prepared to consider separately the merits, and demerits, of these various arrangements. As we do so, a certain inner logic reveals itself in favour of permanence, as also of monogamy. Marital love is inherently exclusive because husband and wife give themselves so completely to each other that they cannot also give themselves to anyone else in the same way. Although polygamy can work, it is under strain. In much the same way, marital love aspires to permanence. Anything less than life-long fidelity is a derogation of true love. Every temporary liaison is impaled on the dilemma that either it was intended to be for keeps, and somebody has been grievously let down by its ending, or it was quite explicit from the outset that it should last only for a season in which case the love that either party bore for the other was not complete. Limited love is a contradiction in terms, and therefore only lasting love is true love.

Some couples intend to stay together for keeps, but do not want to commit themselves irrevocably. They shy away from the shackles of legal obligation, because they think that their union, if it is to subsist at all, must depend solely on their free and unfettered desire that it should continue to exist. But this is to take too high a view of themselves, and to discount unduly the frailty of human affections. Eyes rove, fancy is fickle. Good intentions, without some element of commitment, will not withstand the chances and fleeting irritations of this changing life. If we were more than mere mortal men, intention would be enough to found a marriage on. But in our actual human situation something more than intention is needed, some sense of obligation that will continue, whatever the state of our feelings; and those who seek to lighten the load of mutual obligation are denying to each other the security of pledged commitment. This seems to betoken a lack rather than an excess of perfect love. In other cases the intention itself is only conditional; a couple intend to make a go of it, and will try reasonably hard to make it a success, but they have lurking in their mind that it is only a trial, or that if things don't work out, they can separate without too much difficulty. This is a perfectly possible arrangement, and may be given legal recognition. It is what marriage came to be in ancient Rome, and is believed to be the norm in modern America. But, although it may be a perfectly respectable arrangement, it is not the Christian understanding of marriage, and it is less good. It is untrue to love, and destructive of it. It is untrue to love because neither is giving unreservedly and neither is taking the other unreservedly. There may be *eros* if I move in with you and we share digs together, but there is little or no *agape* if I am taking you only until we have both got our degrees and go our separate ways. We need *agape* more than ever in this anonymous age, when each person is being told by society that he is not an individual but only a type. The promises of the marriage service answer to this need: I take *thee;* not just *a* dolly-bird, *a* typical specimen of twentieth-century womanhood, *a* bed-mate, or *a* serviceable spouse, but *thee, Mary.* It is an individual commitment, and can be fully so only if it is unconditional. If it were conditional, the conditions would define a range of suitable candidates for the job, and the commitment would not be to the person, but to the bearer of suitable qualifications, so that should she cease to be qualified, she might reasonably be traded in for a more satisfactory replacement. Thus in a conditional union I do not take unreservedly: nor do I give unreservedly; all the time I know, or half know, that conditions may arise in which our union may be dissolved, and I shall be on my own again and resume my solo status.

The Christian understanding of marriage is an essentially internal one. It is based not on an observation of the way men and women in society live together and form stable relationships, but on the logic of love and the implications of committing oneself unreservedly to another. The act of commitment is a deliberate affirmation of the first-personal internal view as against the third-personal external one. We know that other people sometimes fall out of love and break up their marriages, but we determine that we shall not follow suit. In the face of the frailty of human feelings we set the determination of our wills, promising that we shall be faithful to each other for better, for worse, till death us do part. This determination is constitutive of our identity. As persons we are shaped by our decisions and the way we stand by them. They enter into our being and make us the persons we are. The commitment to each other in marriage, like the commitment to the Christian faith, is one of those abiding commitments which make us unified persons, and not just bundles of feelings, instincts,

126

opinions, likes and dislikes.[1] Filled out by the shared experiences of life together, and especially of shared sexual experience, it so much enters into our being and makes us the persons we are, that it may be termed an 'ontological' bond, that is to say, a bond of personal *being*. We are made one flesh.[2] Although 'one flesh' has a natural sexual interpretation, taken up by St Paul,[3] it does not mean only that, but carries with it the meaning of kinship. The bond between husband and wife is analogous to, only more fundamental than, the bond between father and son, mother and daughter, or brother and sister. The fact that I have many of the same genes as my father and my mother, my brothers and my sisters, my sons and my daughters, is a fact of life-long significance: and the fact that I have shared not only the same sheets with my wife but the same values, the same hopes and fears, the same aspirations and achievements, the same sorrows and successes, the fact that we have together undertaken to be as one, and to live together until death us do part—this fact too on the Christian view is of profound and continuing significance, profound because of the nature of the marriage bond, and continuing because of the explicit commitment to permanence.

I can never alter the past, but whereas some of my past deeds have spent their significance—the various contracts I have made and fulfilled, the minor social obligations I have discharged—the commitment I made in marriage was total and unreserved, and therefore unconditional, unlimited either by circumstances or by lapse of time. It was unlimited in time, and therefore can never be finished with, and unlimited by circumstances, and therefore can never be cancelled or expunged. I can no more be an ex-husband than I can be an ex-son or an ex-brother: and, whereas it is in the course of nature for sons to leave their parents' homes and for brothers to go their separate ways, my explicit commitment to my wife was to cleave to her, so long as we both shall live.[4]

What can be discerned from the logic of love is confirmed by the teaching of Jesus. Jesus was against divorce. It is possible to understand him as meaning that marriages should not, rather than could not, be dissolved and perhaps allowing for some exceptions; but

[1] John Macquarrie, 'The Nature of the Marriage Bond', *Theology* LXXVIII (May 1975) p. 230.
[1] Gen. 2.24.
[3] I Cor. 6.16.
[4] J. R. Lucas, 'The *Vinculum Conjugale:* a Moral Reality', *Theology* LXXVIII (May 1975) p. 226.

there are good reasons for thinking that Mark's account is closer to the original thought of Jesus than Matthew's, and that the stark simplicity of Luke 16. 18 means what it says. If marriage can be dissolved, then remarriage after divorce is *not* adultery. Only if from a moral and spiritual point of view a person remains married in spite of a legally valid divorce, can remarriage be stigmatised as adultery. On this view, Jesus was not simply laying on us a commandment of obedience, saying that we ought not to divorce and remarry, but was, rather, giving us an understanding of marriage based on the nature of man, which makes divorce impossible and remarriage, therefore, adultery.

It can be further argued, although much more tenuously, that the controversy with the Sadducees about the resurrection of the dead (Matt. 22. 23-33; Mark 12. 18-27; Luke 20. 27-40) would have much greater point if Jesus had maintained that marriages *could* not be dissolved in any circumstances whatsoever. The final judgement, however, is a general one of the nature and meaning of Jesus' teaching and, although there has never been unanimity, 'it remains true', as Lady Oppenheimer allows, 'that the most obvious interpretation of Christ's teaching on marriage is indissolubility of some sort'.[1]

The symbolism of Ephesians 5. 21-32 was used by Augustine to provide a further argument of the indissolubility of marriage. Not only was marriage a *sacramentum* in the secular Latin sense of a solemn commitment which gave rise to permanent obligations, but it was also an outward and visible sign of Christ's love for his Church, and for that reason also it was indissoluble.[2]

In the centuries after Augustine the Western Church developed a more precise and formal sacramental theology, according to which marriage of the baptised was one of the seven sacraments of the Church. It was declared that Jesus himself had raised marriage to the dignity of a sacrament, and that as such it communicated sanctifying grace and established an indissoluble bond between husband and wife. Through the sacrament the love of husband and wife for each other was drawn into the saving mystery of Christ's indestructible love for his Church.

---

[1]Helen Oppenheimer, *The Marriage Bond*, Faith Press, 1976, pp. 53-4; *cf.* 'Is the Marriage Bond an Indissoluble *Vinculum?*' *Theology*, LXXVIII (May 1975) p. 236.
[2]E. Schillebeeckx, *Marriage: Secular Reality and Saving Mystery*, Sheed and Ward, 1965, II, pp. 67-73.

In its marriage discipline, partly under the influence of 1 Corinthians 7. 15. (the 'Pauline privilege'), the Church drew a distinction between marriage of the baptised and marriage of the unbaptised. In both cases the couple made promises which were for life. A contract was thereby established which neither the parties to the marriage themselves nor any other human power had the authority to dissolve. In both cases, therefore, the contract was intrinsically indissoluble. In the case of the unbaptised, however, there were certain circumstances—especially when one of the parties was subsequently baptised and the other refused to continue the marriage—in which the Church claimed the power and authority on behalf of God to dissolve the contract. Thus marriage of the unbaptised, although intrinsically indissoluble, was extrinsically dissoluble. By contrast, sacramental marriage was both intrinsically and extrinsically indissoluble. Once a marriage of the baptised had been duly ratified and consummated, not even the Church had the power and authority to dissolve it. It remained a marriage in all contingencies until death brought it to an end.

Such a doctrine has obvious attractions. It points clearly to the existence and character of a spiritual bond, namely, that of the Spirit of Christ himself. It is the *one* Christ who established the *one* marriage. Nevertheless, the doctrine seems to many to be open to serious criticism. In the eyes of one modern critic, it likens the water of baptism to the hardener which, when subsequently applied, makes the glue of marriage set absolutely hard.[1] More seriously, it enshrines marriage so securely in the order of redemption that it runs the risk of denying its importance in the order of creation. On this view, the marriage at Cana in Galilee would not have been a sacramental marriage, nor would Jesus' teaching be applicable to any of the marriages then existing. Furthermore, the Church of England has always tended to take a non-exclusive view of the Church and of the availability of God's grace. Although Christians may have deeper insights than others into the nature of marriage, the marriage of Christians is not a different sort of thing from any other marriage, and the answer to the question whether a marriage can or cannot be dissolved should not be made to depend on whether the parties have been baptised or not. To reject the traditional Western doctrine of indissolubility, however, is not to deny the value of the insights that lie behind it. As often, criticism of the formulations of earlier ages or of other traditions, lays on us the duty, not of simple rejection, but of

[1] Helen Oppenheimer, *op. cit.*, p. 55.

re-articulating their thoughts so as to express what was valid in them as well as to disown what was invalid.

Although marriage is an institution common to all men and not confined to those admitted to the fellowship of Christ's religion, it has nonetheless a religious aspect. It is the chief source of happiness for men and women, the means whereby they come to know the love of God the Creator. It is also for many men and women a vocation, the special way in which each is called by God the Holy Spirit to make his or her own contribution to the course of history and the working out of God's purposes in the world. And to some the love they have experienced in marriage has represented the love God the Son bore towards his Church. For these reasons it is right to follow Augustine and see parallels to marriage in the sacrament of baptism and the indelibility of Holy Orders. If these were purely human institutions, we should admit that the promises made could be broken, the enterprise fail, and the whole arrangement become nugatory and void. And then, since penitence is always possible and God will never turn away the man who is making a fresh start, we should have the rebaptism of apostates and the re-ordination of priests who had relinquished their orders and subsequently come again to their true vocation and ministry. But we do not. The Church will readmit to the fellowship of faith those who have apostatised after baptism, but will not rebaptise them, because to do so would derogate from the absoluteness of God's commitment to all those baptised into his Church. Baptism is not a purely human institution, an initiation ceremony into the merely visible Church, but a God-given sacrament in which God himself is involved. The impossibility of rebaptism is a mark of its Godward aspect. And although marriage is not a sacrament in the same sense as baptism is, it, too, has a Godward aspect and so the same marks of eternal significance.

To sum up, the doctrine of indissolubility rests on the teaching of Jesus, but not only on that. It takes marriage to be the most fundamental of human relationships, more fundamental than the other, genetic, relationships of family life, and sees it as constitutive of personal identity. It is based on the unalterability of the past, revealing an attitude towards human action that is profoundly serious and moral. Because what I do matters, it matters also what I have done, and I cannot escape from the significance of my past actions except at the cost of making out that nothing I do signifies at all. If we believe that the solemn promises made in marriage do matter and have an eternal significance then we are led to argue that marriage is incapable of being dissolved. But for Christians all these considerations are summed up and sealed by the word of God.

Critics of the indissolubilist position can agree with almost all of what has been said above in its defence. They too acknowledge that Jesus was 'against divorce'. They too see in marriage a fundamental human relationship in which two persons give to each other an identity and a name. They too wish to map out the logic of love and, in so doing, to argue that married love calls for exclusiveness and permanence. They too can affirm the propriety and wisdom of promises of life-long fidelity, to be made with the utmost seriousness of intention and commitment. Furthermore, they themselves are indissolubilists of a kind, in so far as they believe, not only that marriages ought to be indissoluble, but also that in many instances they are *in fact* indissoluble. Why is it, then, when they share so much of the indissolubilist's outlook, that they are unable to take the final step in the argument and assert that marriages can *in no circumstances* be dissolved?

If, as Lady Oppenheimer allows, 'the most obvious interpretation of Christ's teaching on marriage is indissolubility of some sort', nevertheless, as she goes on to affirm, 'what the theory completely loses sight of is the fact that the most obvious interpretation of some aspects of human life is dissolubility of some sort'.[1] Some marriages break down. Personal and social ties are finally and irreparably severed. Must we say, in the light of the teaching of Jesus and of the logic of love, that in some deep and unalterable sense the marriage still exists? Or is the marriage really broken, 'something that stands out as an unnatural smashing of what was built to last, a blasphemy against the unity of Christ and his Church, an amputation inflicted upon a living body'?[2]

Let us take first the teaching of Jesus. What Jesus had in mind cannot be established beyond reasonable doubt. There is more than one way of understanding and interpreting the gospel records. Was he in his condemnation of divorce drawing his hearers back to God's fundamental purpose for marriage, neither endorsing nor repudiating the Mosaic concession to human sin and stupidity? Was he forbidding divorce in all, or at least in most, circumstances, although admitting that men *could* put asunder what God had joined together? Or was he

---

[1]Helen Oppenheimer, *op. cit.*, pp. 53-4.
[2]*Ibid.*, p. 57.

claiming that marriages *could not* be dissolved? To put the question in another way: when Jesus spoke of marriage after divorce as 'adultery', was he speaking literally, thus implying the indissolubility of the marriage bond, or was he bringing together under a single moral condemnation two kinds of action which in themselves remained different and distinct? Detailed discussion of the evidence is to be found in Appendix 4. Critics of the indissolubilist's position maintain that Jesus' words are not to be taken as literally as the indissolubilist suggests: that to do so would be out of accord with the overall sternness *and mercy* of his teaching, and would commit the Church to labelling and treating as adultery *all* subsequent unions after divorce, no matter how loving and stable they might in other respects be.

We turn now to the logic of love. Disagreement centres around the nature and implications of the life-long commitment. For the indissolubilist it is this commitment which is essential to marriage, and it is the integrity of this commitment which must be preserved. His critic does not wish to trivialise this commitment. It is indeed a solemn promise. But what is it a promise of? Is it a promise to remain 'bound' to another person, even when every vestige of caring and sharing has been destroyed? Is that what the words 'for better, for worse' mean? Is it not rather a promise to 'love and to cherish' through good and bad? If, then, it is love that is being pledged for ever and a day, the promise has already lost its substance, whether through breach or through frustration, when all such love and cherishing have perished and there is no possibility of reconciliation and renewal. It is no part of the logic of love to affirm the continued existence of a 'spiritual' bond when love itself has been destroyed.

There remains the unalterable fact that solemn promises were made and lifelong commitment was pledged. A *moral* bond was created, and moral bonds *ought not* to be broken. But when the indissolubilist goes on to affirm that, in the case of marriage, the moral bond is also a spiritual bond and one that *cannot* be broken, his critic cannot agree. It is indeed a very ugly and evil thing to break a solemn promise and commitment such as that expressed in the covenant of marriage. But it is not impossible. And if it is not impossible, then the question must be asked whether there are circumstances in which it is right to acknowledge that the obligation once assumed no longer constrains. The past cannot be undone. Even a second marriage after death of one of the partners to the first marriage can never be the same as a first marriage. But the past may lose its hold on the present, so that marriage after divorce cannot in all cases be ruled out as a moral and spiritual impossibility.

The indissolubilist shares many of his critics' concerns but cannot follow the logic of his argument. It is true that the promises are made for love, and that they need to be worked out and re-authenticated in the love which each shows for the other in the course of their marriage. It is true also that promises can be broken. But breaking a promise does not make it no longer obligatory: moral obligations may be ignored, but they cannot for that reason cease to be binding. And if the promise is construed as conditional upon the continuance of love, it is a different promise, and one which cannot express unconditional commitment and cannot give to a marriage the support which an unconditional commitment can. It is a different understanding of marriage. Although those who put it forward may be propounding a 'high' doctrine of marriage, as were the Jews who followed the teaching of Shammai in Jesus' time, it is not as 'high' as that which teaches that marriages cannot be dissolved. Although the commitment is not the be-all and end-all of marriage, it is a constitutive part, which cannot be soft-pedalled without compromising the whole relationship. A conditional commitment—for better definitely, for worse provided it is not too bad—might seem wiser according to the wisdom of this world, but would lack the unconditionality that is that mark of love, and the utter determination to overcome all adversities that is integral to marriage as seen from the inside. In the end, a complete separation between the first-personal and the third-personal point of view cannot be sustained, and to propound a doctrine of marriage intended to be indissoluble but known to be dissoluble is not just a paradox but a contradiction. When it comes to the point of hard decision, the critics of indissolubility are subordinating the first-personal point of view to the third. This is objectionable not only on the pragmatic ground that it will in all probability weaken the commitment, and thus weaken the whole institution of marriage, but also because it belies the Christian insight that marriage is first and foremost a vocation, a calling which individual men and women respond to by a whole-hearted commitment of themselves in their own persons, supported by the human joy and the divine grace which go to constitute most people's experience of marriage. If it comes to a choice, we must preserve the integrity of men's and women's commitment at all costs, even at that of appearing to be hard on those whose marriages have broken down. There is much that we can do to help them. It may be that they will form another entirely respectable relationship, intended to be permanent and recognised by the civil law, with another partner. If so, Christians should not condemn them, any more than Jesus did. But neither should they blur the distinction between an institution which intends and promises permanence and one which intends it, but promises it only subject to certain conditions. Although the point of entering into the commitment of marriage is to express love, to support a shared life and to nurture a personal relationship, these cannot be made conditions of its validity without undermining it. The reason for having promises and not merely expressions of intent is to import a permanence which purely empirical considerations cannot support. Commitment, therefore is not only an essential element of marriage but is essentially an independent element that stands by itself and does not depend on the continued fulfilment of other conditions for its validity.

The indissolubilist's counter-arguments leave his critic chastened but finally unpersuaded. He is chastened in so far as his criticisms have conveyed the impression that his sights on marriage are 'lower' than those of his fellow Christian who takes the indissolubilist's view. He does not see himself as another Shammai, for he too considers the act of commitment unconditional and does not believe that adultery, or anything else, automatically breaks the bond and renders the commitment null and void. Nevertheless, he cannot isolate the commitment from love—that love which is in its essence a caring and sharing. He does not thereby make the commitment conditional on something other than itself, for the commitment is itself *a commitment to love*. Once committed, husband and wife 'owe' each other love. Herein lies the paradox of marriage, a blending of promise and grace. When, however, through stupidity, blindness or sin a marriage breaks down, and it is no longer possible to continue the commitment to love, to argue that the commitment to the bond of marriage in some separate and independent sense continues to be obligatory without possibility of cancellation is to tighten the logic of promise-making until it snaps. The indissolubilist accuses his critic of substituting, in the end, a conditional promise for an unconditional commitment. His critic replies that, in the end, the indissolubilist has substituted an abstract principle for the concrete realities of life and love.

Marriage is a vocation and a venture. The indissolubilist and his critic both wish to affirm its permanence and to point to its eternal significance. The indissolubilist sees the ground of permanence in the act of commitment. Although in one sense marriages are always in the making, in another sense, once made, they are always made. What is promised is already effected. His critic, on the other hand, cannot place so great a weight on commitment or on the past. Important though these are, the continuing union of love in the present and into the future are equally if not more important. What is promised in faith has still to be realised in fact. Eternity has to be fashioned through time. Time can, through human weakness and sin, unmake eternity. Even a solemn and unconditional commitment can in certain circumstances cease to bind. He affirms this as a paradox. The indissolubilist rejects it as a contradiction.

4
The New Testament Evidence

INTRODUCTION
In making this report we have had to bear in mind the criticisms which were levelled against the Root Report. In particular the presentation of the New Testament evidence was severely criticised. The relegation of this evidence to an appendix was held to imply that the teaching of Jesus was only of secondary importance. The presentation of material was said to be 'far too influenced by one particular school of New Testament scholarship'.[1] The interpretation of the words of Jesus was criticised as reaching a conclusion contrary to their plain meaning, and suspiciously close to the main recommendation of the Report as a whole. The Report was published at a time when there was a widespread feeling in the popular mind that the work of scholars had dissolved all hope of reaching back behind the gospels to the historical Jesus, so that his teaching could not be recovered with certainty. It was felt by some critics that the Appendix was calculated to confirm such extreme scepticism.

It is not our purpose to defend the Root Report against these criticisms, though this does not mean that we consider them to be justified. Rather, we hope that readers of this report will be able to see for themselves that we have paid careful attention to them, and that we are aware of the fears which often lie behind them. We have tried to understand the teaching of Jesus, and to hold fast by it.

In what follows an attempt will be made to set out the teaching of Jesus on marriage which is contained in the gospels and to draw out the implications of it. It has to be remembered that Jesus spoke in a setting where the Jewish law was operative. It was taken for granted that marriage was a permanent union. The law did, however, permit (or even require) divorce by the husband in certain circumstances. The grounds on which this law might be invoked were hotly disputed in the time of Jesus. Women had no legal right to institute divorce proceedings although in some cases they were able, in effect, to secure for themselves a divorce. Jesus certainly upheld the permanence of marriage and expressed disapproval of the practice of divorce in his day. Thus far his attitude is comparable to that of the Qumran

[1]The Bishop of Truro in his Presidential Address to the Truro Diocesan Synod, May 1974.

Community and no doubt of other reforming groups.[1] Whether he also assumed the role of lawgiver and abrogated the divorce law of Deuteronomy 24.1 is disputed. In general it is clear that he promoted the highest ethical standard among his followers. He even appears to have commended celibacy for those consecrated to the work of the gospel, remaining unmarried himself. Contrary to public belief, celibacy was by no means unknown in Judaism of the time.[2] Paul also appears to have followed the Master in remaining unmarried (though some think that he was a widower) and in commending celibacy. But Paul has much of positive value to say, and so our survey will conclude with an attempt to relate his teaching to that of Jesus.

THE WORDS OF JESUS

The relevant sayings in the gospels are few, but the relations between them are complex. Matthew has sayings on adultery (Matt. 5. 27-28) and on divorce (Matt. 5. 31-32) in the Sermon on the Mount. He also has a dispute between Jesus and the Pharisees about divorce, which is found also in Mark (Matt. 19 3-8 = Mark 10. 2-9). This ends with another saying on divorce (Matt. 19. 9 = Mark 10. 10-12). It is followed in Matthew only by a unique saying on celibacy (eunuchs for the kingdom of heaven's sake, Matt. 19. 10-12). Mark has no further relevant material. Luke has nothing but a saying on divorce (Luke 16. 18). In addition, the question of the Sadducees about the resurrection, which is found in all three gospels, has implications for Jesus' understanding of marriage (Matt. 22. 23-33 = Mark 12. 18-27 = Luke 20. 27-40). There are no relevant texts in John.[3]

---

[1]For prophetic protest against divorce, cf. Mal. 2. 13-16. For Qumran, cf. the Damascus Document (CD 4.20-5.5), where Gen. 1. 27 is quoted against polygamy (cf. Mark 10. 7).

[2]References to the Essenes in Philo, Josephus and the elder Pliny all agree that they were celibate, but Josephus asserts that some were married (Jewish War ii. 121). Marriage was allowed at Qumran, but the community's way of life presupposes celibacy as the norm.

[3]There is an exception, if John 4. 18 is considered to be relevant. Here the Samaritan woman has claimed to have no husband, but Jesus knows this to be untrue: 'You are right in saying, "I have no husband"; for you have had five husbands, and he whom you now have is not your husband; this you said truly' (John 4. 17-18). This could mean that though the woman is properly married according to the law, Jesus refuses to regard her as married because he does not recognise her previous divorces. On this interpretation the passage reflects Jesus' disapproval of divorce and perhaps implies a doctrine of indissolubility. Alternatively Jesus might have allowed up to three divorces, in common with a known rabbinic opinion, but regarded any more as reprehensible. This would explain why five husbands are mentioned. This would not necessarily have been his real opinion, because he speaks throughout this passage from the standpoint of Jewish attitudes towards the Samaritans, simply as a basis of argument. This means that he keeps his own opinion covered. A third possibility is that Jesus means the words literally: the woman has been divorced five times, and is now living with a man to whom she is not legally married. Finally the words are often taken allegorically, so that the woman's 'husband' is her Samaritan religion, which is impure from a Jewish point of view.

(a) *The saying on adultery*

After citing the commandment against adultery, Jesus gives his own teaching: 'But I say to you that every one who looks at a woman lustfully has already committed adultery with her in his heart' (Matt. 5. 28). The saying expresses Jesus' characteristic concern for purity of heart and honesty with oneself before God. This must be remembered as a prime motive in his teaching on marriage and divorce. It also illustrates a striking feature of his ethical teaching with regard to method. He intends to say that the lustful glance is morally equivalent to adultery, but he speaks as if it were actually identical.

(b) *The sayings on divorce*

These must be considered together, because they express the same thought in various ways, but appear to be adapted to suit different circumstances. Many scholars hold that they stem from one original saying, which has been transmitted independently through at least two channels of tradition.

Matt. 5. 31-32. The framework is similar to the preceding saying on adultery. Jesus first refers to the law of Deut. 24. 1, which gives regulations in the case of a man who wishes to divorce his wife 'because he has found some indecency in her'.[1] He then gives his own teaching: 'But I say to you that every one who divorces his wife, except on the ground of unchastity, makes her an adulteress; and whoever marries a divorced woman commits adultery'. Comparison with the saying on adultery suggests that the point of Jesus' teaching is that divorce and remarriage (divorce without remarriage is not here in question) are morally equivalent to adultery, rather than actually identical with it. This interpretation presupposes that Jesus here makes a moral judgement on the scandalous way in which men use the law of Deuteronomy, rather than enacts a new law which abrogates it. This question will be considered in greater detail in connection with the dispute with the Pharisees about divorce in (c) below.

There is, however, a further difficulty of interpretation in the famous Matthaean exception. The Greek phrase here (but not in Matt.

---

[1]The meaning of the phrase translated 'some indecency' (*'erwath dabhar*, literally 'nakedness of a thing') is uncertain, and so left room for widely varying interpretations. Shammai confined it to adultery by the woman, but Hillel applied it to almost anything that a husband might dislike in his wife, including his disgust with her poor cooking or his preference for another woman. Hillel's easygoing attitude shows scant regard for women. From this point of view Shammai's ruling is more just and humane, and it is not surprising that this is the one point where Jesus appears to agree with Shammai against Hillel.

138

19. 9, where it is *mē epi porneia* = 'except for unchastity') is *parektos logou porneias*, which may be translated 'apart from a matter of unchastity' or 'apart from the reason of unchastity'. This appears to be an attempt to represent the Hebrew phrase of Deut. 24. 1. If so, it is natural to conclude that this law was accepted as normative in the Matthaean church. If the exception is a Matthaean addition, and not an authentic part of the underlying words of Jesus, it may be concluded further that it has been inserted as a result of the debate on the meaning of the phrase in Deut. 24. 1 between the rival schools of Hillel and Shammai. Then the translation of the Hebrew *'erwāh* = 'sexual uncleanness' by the Greek *porneia* = 'unlawful sexual intercourse' indicates that Matthew sides with the school of Shammai in maintaining a strict interpretation of the Deuteronomic law, confining the legitimate cause of divorce to the woman's adultery. This agrees in fact with the traditional interpretation. Both the Eastern Orthodox churches and the churches of the Protestant Reformation have allowed divorce on the grounds of adultery, assuming that the exception goes back to Jesus himself, and that this is what he meant by *porneia*.

It seems, then, that the Matthaean exception decisively affects the interpretation of the saying on divorce. The saying cannot be intended to exclude divorce altogether, if the grounds for divorce given in Deut. 24. 1 are specifically upheld. Those who hold that the exception is an addition by the evangelist, and does not go back to Jesus himself, are free to believe that Jesus intended to abrogate the Deuteronomic law altogether, and that Matthew has significantly modified the meaning of the saying by introducing the exception. In any case, if the words are an addition, it is clear that Matthew is treating the saying as law, in a setting where the Jewish law remains operative among Christians, whether the saying itself was a legal enactment or not.

This is not the end of the matter. In recent years a new interpretation of *porneia* has been put forward, which has the effect of making the Matthaean exception equivalent to nullity (of course the Bible makes no formal distinction between nullity and dissolution from a legal point of view). It has been pointed out that the proper Hebrew equivalent, *zenūth*, is used in rabbinic discussions with a specialised, almost technical, sense to refer to marriage within the forbidden degrees of consanguinity, as laid down in Leviticus 18. This was a live issue in the time of Christ, because Gentile converts to Judaism might already be married within the forbidden degrees. On this view the Matthaean exception in no way modifies Jesus' prohibition of divorce, because it only excludes what is in any case forbidden. But it must be pointed out that very few who hold this view actually ascribe the exception to Jesus, as it is very unlikely that he would make special reference to this point of detail in the course of challenging and provocative teaching to a Jewish audience who would wholeheartedly approve of it without being personally affected by it. On the other hand, if the exception is an addition by Matthew, this interpretation makes a great deal of sense, as his church could not escape the problems raised by the accession of Gentiles to Christianity and would certainly have required the application of the Jewish rules to any whose marital status was unacceptable.

It may be said in favour of this interpretation of *porneia* that it is very well suited to the implications of the apostolic decrees (Acts 15. 20, 29; 21. 25), which lay down minimal Jewish rules to be observed by Gentile Christians without becoming proselytes. It also saves our present verse (Matt. 5. 32) from the apparent self-contradiction of allowing the law of Deut. 24. 1 at the same time as claiming to supersede it. On the other side it may be urged that *porneia* is a common word with a broad range of meaning, and the reader can be expected to understand it in this specialised sense only if there is some indication in the context. This applies in the case of the apostolic decrees in Acts, but not in Matthew. But, even if this interpretation is right in Matthew, it remains difficult to ascribe the exception to Jesus himself, so that once more the addition has to be attributed to the application of the saying of Jesus to legal situations in the Matthean church.[1]

Matt. 19. 9 = Mark 10. 10-12. These parallel forms of the saying on divorce can be dealt with more briefly. Mark's version shows clearly that it is a separate unit of tradition from the dispute between Jesus and the Pharisees which immediately precedes it. The point is made in uncompromising fashion: 'Whoever divorces his wife and marries another, commits adultery against her; and if she divorces her husband and marries another, she commits adultery'. It is widely held that the second part of the saying is an addition, expanding the original, because it presupposes the wife's right to divorce her

---

[1]Another recent interpretation of the Matthaean exception is that it refers to premarital fornication by the woman during the period of betrothal. In this case it would be necessary to stop the marriage, and the contract, not yet completed, would have to be annulled. This has the same advantages, and is open to the same objections, as the other interpretation, and appears far less likely.

husband, which was not the case in Judaism. Thus Mark's version has been expanded to meet the needs of the church in a Gentile setting. However this latter part may be an adaptation rather than an addition (see below on Luke 16. 18). The first part can certainly lay claim to reproduce the teaching of Jesus. In Matthew the saying is an integral part of the preceding dispute story, and we shall have to consider it again in that context. For the moment we may observe that he reproduces only the first part of the saying as it appears in Mark, but significantly adds 'except for unchastity'. If Matthew is here dependent upon Mark, it can be asserted with confidence that he has made both these changes to suit the conditions of his Jewish-Christian church. Alternatively Mark may be adapting Matthew for the sake of his Gentile church, or both may be independent adaptations from a common original.

Luke 16. 18. Luke omits the dispute story, and has this saying as an isolated unit, not at all well fitted to its present context: 'Every one who divorces his wife and marries another commits adultery, and he who marries a woman divorced from her husband commits adultery'. This is very similar to Mark's saying, but, by dealing with marriage to a divorced woman rather than the marriage of a woman who has divorced her husband, it keeps within the conditions of the Jewish law. In this respect it stands closer to Matt. 5. 32, and indeed the Greek phraseology is closer. On the other hand the Matthaean exception is not included. Moreover there is no diminution of the stark moral thrust of the Markan version. There is thus much to be said for the view that Luke's version is nearest to the original form of the saying.[1] If so, the saying must have been transmitted separately from Mark's version and Luke has not derived it from Matt. 5. 32, which is then to be regarded as dependent on it before it came to Luke. On this showing the saying on divorce has been transmitted in two channels of tradition, one of which lies behind Matt. 5. 32 and Luke 16. 18 (which has best preserved the original form), and the other behind Mark 10. 11-12 and Matt. 19. 9. If this is right, it gives to the saying double attestation, and makes the essential agreement between the various versions all the more important. Other

---

[1]Montefiore (*Marriage, Divorce and the Church*, p. 88) argues against this on the grounds that Luke 16. 18 is too dissimilar to Matt. 5. 32 for both sayings to be taken from a common document (the hypothetical 'Q' source). This is too rigid a view of the 'Q' tradition, part of which is extremely close, with only the slightest verbal differences between Matthew and Luke, but other parts vary so widely that the differences cannot be ascribed only to the individual evangelists.

explanations of the relationship between them inevitably lead to a lower valuation of the Lukan form.

Despite these complications, it seems clear that Jesus made an uncompromising statement about divorce: a man or woman who remarries after divorce commits adultery. In Matthew the two forms of the saying are both in contexts which refer to the law of Deut. 24. 1 (i.e. Matt. 5. 31 and 19. 7), and so permit the interpretation that Jesus formally abrogates that law. On this interpretation his words in the saying mean that remarriage after divorce actually is adultery. This could be the intention of Mark, inasmuch as he has brought the saying into relation with the dispute story, though without integrating the two as closely as Matthew. It is obvious, however, that this interpretation depends on the assumption that in the dispute story Jesus in fact does abrogate the Deuteronomic law, and this is by no means certain. Hence, even in these contexts, it does not necessarily follow that the saying is intended to mean that remarriage after divorce is actually identical with adultery. The alternative interpretation, that Jesus means that such remarriage is morally equivalent to adultery, is equally possible.

This possibility is supported by Luke. Not only does he omit the dispute story altogether. He even implies that the saying is not intended to alter the law by placing it immediately after the words: 'But it is easier for heaven and earth to pass away, than for one dot of the law to become void' (Luke 16. 17).

The view that Jesus is making a comparison in no way reduces the moral force of the saying. Speaking from within the setting of the Jewish law, Jesus could only be understood to be making a severe comment on abuse of the law. But it would simply not be true that one who acted within the letter of the law was legally an adulterer.

(c) *The dispute about divorce*

This story is crucial for the discussion of Jesus' intentions, for it is the only place in the gospels where it is claimed that he not only radicalised the law but actually rescinded a provision of it. On this view Jesus treated the law of Deut. 24. 1 as if it had only the same status as the tradition of the elders, which, according to Mark 7. 8, he rejected in order that the commandment of God should not be evaded. This view has always held the field, because on a high Christology there never seemed to be any reason to doubt that Jesus might replace the law with a new law consistent with a fuller revelation. However, the alternative view, that Jesus did not abrogate the law of Deut. 24.

1, is equally consistent with a high Christology and a fuller revelation; and the reason why it has been promoted in recent study is not that there has been a weakening of Christology but that the study of the sayings of Jesus has been undertaken with a finer historical sense.

The story is preserved in Matt. 19. 3-8(9) and Mark 10. 2-9. The two versions are so closely related that dependence of one of them on the other is difficult to deny. Nevertheless there are very important differences between them.

In Matthew the Pharisees ask Jesus for a ruling on the conditions in which a man may divorce his wife. Is it permissible 'for any cause'? In his reply Jesus first states God's intention that marriage should be permanent, adducing two fundamental texts (Gen. 1. 27 and 2. 24) and concluding with the comment: 'What therefore God has joined together, let no man put asunder'. His opponents then object that the law of Deut. 24. 1 commands (*eneteilato*) divorce in certain circumstances. Jesus replies that this law is permissive (*epetrepsen*) rather than mandatory, and that this was not God's original intention. He then adds the saying on divorce, which we have already considered above (Matt. 19. 9). In the context it means that only 'unchastity' may be accepted as a ground for divorce, and all other causes must be rejected as leading to legalised adultery.

It will be seen from this summary that Matthew's version does not preclude the use of the existing law of Deut. 24. 1. Rather it seeks to reduce its use and to limit its scope. This is consistent with his position in Matt. 5. 32. Matthew wishes to promote Jesus' teaching on purity of heart and the permanence of the marriage bond, but he does not presuppose that the law must be changed in order to do so.

The other interpretations of the Matthaean exception (that it refers to the marriage of Gentiles within the forbidden degrees, or to fornication during the period of betrothal) do not basically alter the argument, though they make Matthew's position more rigorous. They simply limit the grounds of divorce to situations which were in any case so offensive to Jewish sensibility that no one would dispute the application of the law in these cases. It may be said in favour of these interpretations that the complaint of the disciples which immediately follows in Matt. 19. 10 ('if such is the case of a man with his wife, it is not expedient to marry') presupposes a rigorous demand.

In Mark the question is whether resort may be made to the law permitting divorce at all. It thus has to be presupposed that Jesus is known to teach a high view of the marriage bond. Precisely because the law does permit divorce, his opponents see the opportunity afforded by this issue to trap him into denying the law. It is for this reason that it is most improbable that he actually did so. The whole point of the story is that Jesus maintained his position without falling into the trap. Mark makes this perfectly clear by pointing out that, in asking their question, the opponents of Jesus did so 'in order to test him' (Mark 10. 2, *cf.* Matt. 19. 3). Well aware of their intentions, Jesus throws the question back at them, and they cite Deut. 24. 1. Jesus then shows that this law, which he acknowledges to be a commandment (*entole*), is only concessionary, because it cannot undermine the principle enunciated in Gen. 1. 27 and 2. 24, that the union of the sexes is a divine ordinance in the order of creation. He then adds his own comment, as in Matthew, underlining the importance of Gen. 2. 24 and drawing his own conclusion from it: 'So they are no longer two but one flesh.[1] What therefore God has joined together, let not man put asunder'. With this pronouncement Jesus makes recourse to divorce morally impossible without denying the legal validity of the law of Deut. 24. 1.

To avoid misunderstanding, it must be pointed out that 'flesh' in this context, as often in Hebrew, refers to kinship. What Gen. 2. 24 means is that, in marriage, a man leaves the family home and creates a new kinship unit. It is the conclusion to the story of the creation of Eve out of Adam's rib. This story accounts for the phenomenon of sexual attraction, which results in the practice (assumed by the writer to be universal) of the creation of a new home when a man takes a wife from another home. Thus Gen. 2. 24 states a general truth rather than a command. It does not provide any guidance on the question of divorce, though in the absence of other evidence it would seem to imply a lasting union, and this is how Jesus takes it. Nor does it necessarily lay emphasis on sexual intercourse, as if failure to consummate a marriage might be grounds for nullity, because it is the leaving of the parental home in order to set up a new kinship nucleus which makes the marriage. In fact this text is capable of a variety of interpretations, and as such makes the starting point for any Jewish teaching about marriage.[2]

---

[1] RSV, followed here, omits 'flesh' from the text, and relegates it to the margin. This is to avoid the impression that the union referred to is only a matter of sexual intercourse (as explained in the next paragraph).

[2] In rabbinic texts Gen. 2. 24 is quoted as authority for the avoidance of incest, and indeed in connection with all problems of consanguinity, and also as the authority for heterosexual relations (against pederasty and sexual perversions). As a text regarded as normative for rulings on marriage, it is not surprising to find it quoted again in the New Testament in I Cor. 6. 16 and Eph. 5. 31 independently.

144

Finally, Jesus' conclusion, that what God joined man should not put asunder, does not imply that the law of Deut. 24. 1 is a man-made law which has wrongfully undermined the law of God. The man who is referred to here is any man who invokes this law, not Moses who enacted it. It thus seems that Jesus is saying that the law stands, but nobody has any right to use it. Before we dismiss this as absurd, we should remember that ironical exaggeration is characteristic of Jesus' moral challenge. His aim was to promote a high ideal of marriage, in line with the high ethical standards which, according to his teaching, alone belong to the kingdom of God. His appeal was to the conscience, not to the letter of the law.

Nevertheless, this conclusion of Jesus has traditionally been taken to be the enunciation of a new law. But this is possible only because the true nature of the story goes unrecognised. Once it is seen that Jesus' opponents are hoping to trap Jesus into denying a prescription of law, it can scarcely be maintained that he actually did so. It then follows that Jesus' conclusion, concise and epigrammatic as it is, cannot be a new law replacing the old. It can be argued, however, that this is in effect what it is, so that it is properly accepted as law in the Christian community, where in any case the Jewish law is superseded. But this is to anticipate the transition from precept to law.

(d) *The question about the resurrection*
This is another story in which an attempt is made to trap Jesus. It is recorded in all three synoptic gospels (Matt. 22. 23-33; Mark 12. 18-27; Luke 20. 27-40), but the differences between them are not significant for our present purpose. In this case the issue is not marriage as such, but the teaching of Jesus on personal resurrection in the coming kingdom. His views on this subject do not seem to have been different from those of the Pharisees, who promoted the doctrine of resurrection as leaders of popular piety. The conservative and aristocratic Sadducees resisted it, along with other popular developments of the time. But there was no clearly defined doctrine, and opinions varied from crudely naïve and literalistic ideas of resurrection life, which were ridiculed by the Sadducees, to the more spiritual views found in the teaching of Jesus.

In this story the Sadducees set up a hypothetical case which, from a literalistic point of view, would be manifestly absurd. According to the law of levirate marriage (Deut. 25. 5-6) the inheritance of a man who died without an heir could be secured if his widow bore a son to his brother. The case is imagined of a woman who had a series of unions with seven brothers in the hope of saving her husband's inheritance, and then found herself in the resurrection life with all seven as husbands. The point of the story is that the law of Deut. 25. 5-6 presupposes that marriage is ended by death. The woman no longer has her husband. But if the dead are raised, he will still be alive, and so it can be argued that the woman will not be free to marry his brother as the law requires.

Thus there is a discrepancy between the implications of the law of God and the natural assumptions of those who believe in resurrection. Jesus solves the problem by asserting that there is no such thing as marriage in the resurrection life, but men will be 'like angels'. The boundaries of physical marriage are transcended in the conditions of the coming kingdom.[1]

There is a real issue here, however ridiculous the Sadducees make it seem. The early church holding firmly to the doctrine of resurrection, might have been expected to refuse the marriage of a widow or widower on the grounds that the first marriage was not ended. It is thus all the more significant that Paul accepts the legal position without demur, and duly allows widows to marry again (I Cor. 7. 39). He advises them to remain unmarried, but that is not because the first marriage is not ended, but because of his strong preference for celibacy.

(e) *The saying on celibacy*

From the material which we have studied so far it has become clear

---

[1]In the interpretation given in the text it is presupposed that resurrection is the main point at issue. The Sadducees try to trap Jesus into denying a provision of the law which in their view does not allow for resurrection. The fact that the provision is concerned with marriage is from this point of view incidental. This is borne out by the reply of Jesus, who goes on to cite another passage of the law (Exodus 3. 6), which supports the doctrine of resurrection but is not concerned with marriage. But it is possible to maintain that Jesus' teaching on marriage is central to the argument. On this interpretation Jesus' opposition to divorce implies a doctrine of indissolubility; and if the dead are raised, the marriage is not dissolved by death. But the levirate law requires dissolution of the first marriage, and if this is not achieved by death it will have to be done by some equivalent of divorce. Thus, whereas in the dispute with the Pharisees Jesus could confirm the validity of the divorce law of Deut. 24. 1 and at the same time tell people not to use it, because it was only concessionary, in this case he can be expected to refuse a provision which the law positively requires. In his reply Jesus shows that the continuation of the marriage after death does not entail the need for dissolution in order to carry out the levirate law. It will be seen that this interpretation presupposes that the Sadducees wish to challenge Jesus on two issues, not one. Ostensibly they wish to refute his teaching on resurrection, which he shares with the Pharisees; but in fact they also wish to side with the Pharisees in resisting his opposition to divorce. It is a weakness of this interpretation that the latter issue is not brought out in the text.

that Jesus' concept of purity of heart embraced not only fidelity in marriage and the avoidance of lust, but also the transcending of marriage in the resurrection life. We come now finally to the one saying in the gospels in which Jesus recommends celibacy (Matt. 19. 10-12). The authenticity of the saying has been doubted on the grounds that it appears to be casuistic, defining different classes of 'eunuchs', and also because Jesus is regarded as unlikely to differ from the customary Jewish outlook which regards marriage as an obligation. But, as already pointed out, it is wrong to suppose that celibacy as an ideal was unknown among the Jews at this time. There are really no compelling grounds to dispute the saying. As celibacy is commended to 'those who can receive it', and thus not to everyone, it is natural to assume that the original application of the saying was to the apostles themselves, who have either renounced marriage or left wife and family in order to assist Jesus, himself celibate, in his eschatological mission. For such renunciation we may compare Matt. 19. 29, and parallels in Mark and Luke, in which Jesus promises rewards to those who have left family and possessions for the sake of the gospel (it is uncertain, however, whether the list of renunciations included 'wife' in the original form of the saying). It is thus at least possible that Jesus counselled celibacy for those consecrated to the message of the gospel, and this adds to the impression that his attitudes, if they were not ascetic, were nonetheless marked by spiritualised ideals.

FROM PRECEPT TO LAW

The ethics of Jesus are radical, spontaneous, generous and free. The primitive church evinced these qualities, derived from the inspiration of his leadership. As in all movements of the spirit, geographical expansion and the passage of time brought the need to accommodate the way of life to more conventional patterns and to reduce the precepts of Jesus to manageable rules. But this was not necessarily a matter of lowering standards. Conscious of their high calling, the early Christians tended to regard the precepts of Jesus as the rules of their society, and in this way treated them as laws.

We have already seen this process at work in the gospels. In Mark 10. 12 there appears to be some degree of adaptation of the saying on divorce to meet the needs of Christians in pagan setting, where women had the legal right to divorce their husbands. The saying, perhaps intended as we have seen to be a comparison, allows the

147

interpretation that remarriage after divorce actually is adultery. This may well have been the view of Christians faced with the greater laxity of a pagan society at the time when Mark was writing, just as it certainly became the normal interpretation of the verse at a later time.

In Matthew the exception for *porneia* (however this is interpreted) indicates that the saying is regarded as an absolute rule, so that the boundaries of its application have to be defined. On the traditional view of the exception it had to be conceded that the Matthaean church permitted Christians to use the Jewish law of divorce, but only within the limits of a strict interpretation of it. Thus, on any showing, every effort is made to maintain the spirit of the teaching of Jesus.

Paul in I Corinthians gives the most important evidence for the practical application of Jesus' teaching on marriage. Written before any of the gospels, this letter vividly portrays the difficulties of maintaining the ethical ideals of Jesus in the permissive society of a pagan city. Paul's careful discrimination between the precepts which he has received from the tradition of Jesus' teaching and his own rulings shows that he was faced with problems which were entirely new, requiring decisions for which there was no precedent.

(a) *I Corinthians 7*

Paul begins by insisting on the moral necessity for stable, monogamous unions. His concern for the avoidance of immorality (verse 2) stems from Jesus' own teaching on purity of heart. His personal celibacy and recommendation of it to others (verses 7-9) accord with Jesus' own practice, the saying about eunuchs, and the implications of the reply to the question about resurrection. His charge not to divorce (verses 10-11) takes into account the right of women in pagan Corinth to divorce their husbands. Neither men nor women in the Christian brotherhood are to exercise this right by command of the Lord. Paul here may well be referring to the actual saying of Jesus on divorce which we have considered in various forms above.

Next comes the unprecedented situation which is resolved by the 'Pauline privilege' (verses 12-16). Here again Paul has to take into account the fact that an unbelieving wife may initiate proceedings against her husband just as much as the other way round. In either case the believing partner is powerless to stop the separation, however much it may go against Christian principles. Paul argues for the continuance of the marriage if possible, but not on the grounds that

148

divorce in such a case is necessarily wrong, but because it provides a missionary opportunity. Unfortunately he does not say whether those whose marriages are dissolved in these circumstances are free to marry again. Nevertheless this may be the implication of verse 15, where he says that such a person 'is not bound' (*dedoulotai*, literally 'enslaved'). In this case it may be significant that he does not here repeat the prohibition of remarriage made in connection with the separation of Christians in verse 11.

Paul's teaching in this chapter cannot be properly understood without reference to the situation in Corinth to which his remarks are addressed. At first sight it seems that Paul wishes to promote celibacy as far as possible, so that he has a rather grudging attitude towards marriage. In fact he is much more positive than this. He certainly has a preference for celibacy, and it can be safely assumed that he has passed this on in his previous teaching to the Corinthians. But it is they who have taken it to extremes. So now he has to correct this onesidedness, but without going to the opposite extreme of decrying celibacy which he values so highly. The chapter is thus a sort of balancing act. He has to insist on the rightness of marriage for those who are free to marry and wish to do so, at the same time as wishing that they would remain single.

In the case of the person with an unbelieving partner, which we have just considered, the situation presupposed is not merely the unbelieving partner's action but also pressure on the part of the Corinthians for the couples to separate and the believing partner to live the celibate life. Paul puts all his energy into stopping this. Mixed marriages should not be broken up. He underlines the point by explaining that as a general rule converts should continue in the same condition as before their conversion (verses 17-24). This applies equally to circumcised Jews and to slaves. Each person's status is his calling from God, and entry into the church does not alter it.

After this Paul turns to the position of Christians who are unmarried at the time of their conversion (verses 25-38). The word he actually uses is 'virgins' (*tōn parthenōn*), but the grammatical form can be either masculine or feminine, and it is probably intended to mean people of either sex who have never been married. As before (*cf.* verse 8) he recommends celibacy. But he is careful to make it clear that this is his own advice, not a 'command of the Lord'. The basic principle is the one just enunciated, that conversion should not necessarily lead to change of condition, so that the married in general should not seek to be separated and the unmarried in general should not seek to be wedded. But for the latter case Paul actually says 'free from a wife' (*lelusai apo gunaikos*, verse 27), which at first sight seems to refer to widowers or divorced men (both kinds are likely to have been among the converts), but must include bachelors as well. It can be argued from this that Paul regards those who have been divorced before their conversion as having the same status as others who are unmarried at the time of their conversion. All such people are in Paul's view entitled to get married, contrary to the prevailing opinion at Corinth, though he would prefer them not to do so (verse 28a).

At this point Paul enlarges on the reason for this preference. It is because the time is short, and Christians will need to devote all their attention to surviving the ordeal which precedes the transition to the heavenly existence (verses 29-35). This argument must be taken seriously. It is altogether wrong to suppose that, because Paul says that marriage will lead to worldly troubles (verse 28b), he has a jaundiced view of marriage and is unconsciously giving expression to his own sexual frustration. Contrary to popular belief, there is no firm evidence that he had an unhealthy and inhibited attitude towards sex. But his teaching, like that of all the early Christians, was set in the context of a foreshortened eschatological perspective. Believing that the transition from worldly to heavenly existence was already coming to pass (verse 31), his first concern was to promote the kind of behaviour which belongs to that existence. The actual transition for each person would be through resurrection (argued at length in I Cor. 15), and this would not be long delayed (I Thess. 4. 13-5. 11). And, as Jesus had himself said, 'when they rise from the dead, they neither marry nor are given in marriage, but are like angels in heaven' (Mark 12. 25). We cannot, obviously, take this view today without considerable qualifications. But it is necessary to see that it was Paul's view, because otherwise we cannot do justice to his teaching. The reiterated emphasis on celibacy is due to Paul's understanding of the resurrection life, derived from Jesus himself. The only difficulty is that the Corinthians have accepted this teaching too enthusiastically, and decided that no one in the Church should be married at all. But Paul sees very clearly that, even if marriage is not the form of life for the coming kingdom, those who are married will best prepare for the heavenly life by following their calling faithfully and lovingly. There is bound to be some tension, however, because marriage is a 'worldly' institution (i.e. belongs to the present order of existence) and what is

150

being prepared for is an existence in which the relationships between persons will have a different form. Consequently Paul does not want to bring any pressure to bear on people not to be married, but only wants to point out that the unmarried way is less complicated (verse 35).

Paul still has not quite finished with those who are unmarried at the time of their conversion. There is the case of virgins who are on the brink of marriage, but might feel bound to remain celibate in view of this teaching (verses 36-38). Though the exact situation is not clear, it seems best to assume that Paul is speaking of betrothed couples, whose sexual instincts are strongly aroused, and who could only with the greatest difficulty break off the engagement. No disgrace is to attach to them if they do go ahead and get married.[1]

The chapter ends with advice to widows (verses 39-40). Paul is here dealing, not with people's marital situation at the time of their conversion, but with situations which may be expected to arise in the course of the Christian life. It is not surprising to find, in view of the above argument, that Paul agrees with Jesus in accepting the legal position that marriage is ended by death. Hence remarriage is permissible, provided that it is undertaken responsibly as a Christian ('in the Lord'), even though it is obviously not ideal from Paul's point of view, and of most of the Corinthians themselves.[2]

In this chapter Paul is making rules for the Christian community, which requires a higher moral standard than the law of the land. The precepts of Jesus naturally provide the basis for his decisions. They are the norms, and are on the way to becoming laws. But it would be an anachronism to speak of this development as a church law, having the same status as the civil law, whether Jewish or Roman. Paul forbids divorce on the authority of Jesus, but he does not provide any guidance for dealing with cases where divorce between Christians

---

[1]An older view is that these are virgins under parental care, who are restrained from marriage by their fathers beyond the normal marriageable age, so that the man in the passage is the father or guardian and not the bridegroom. But this is so confusing that it leaves the reader wondering who is marrying whom. An alternative view is that the passage refers to a couple who have entered upon a spiritual marriage, in which they are vowed to abstain from physical relations. Though such arrangements are known at a later time, there is no other evidence for them in New Testament times, and Paul's attitude to marriage earlier in the chapter suggests that he would not have approved of such arrangements.

[2]Paul states the same position in a more straightforward way in Rom. 7. 1-3, in order to illustrate his argument on the death to sin and new birth to righteousness. He confines attention to wives, because husbands can in fact gain freedom in the lifetime of their partners by the Jewish law of divorce, whereas this does not apply to women.

actually occurs, except to urge the divorcees to remain unmarried or to be reconciled to one another (verse 11). Whether any who insisted on making a fresh marriage would have been excluded from the Christian fellowship is not stated (contrast chapter 5).

(b) *I Corinthians 6. 16*
The chapter which we have just surveyed is concerned with practical aspects of marriage, but gives little indication of the theology of it. However Paul has already given a hint of his thinking on this subject in dealing with fornication in the preceding chapter. His point is that membership of Christ requires that the disciple bring himself wholly into obedience to Christ, not just part of himself. It is thus not possible to give one's body (*sōma*) to a harlot and at the same time to be true to one's membership in Christ. To drive home the argument Paul quotes part of Gen. 2. 24: 'The two shall become one flesh (*sarx*)'. Evidently he is arguing against a libertine tendency among some Corinthians, who suggested that bodily indulgence was not inconsistent with dedication to Christ. He replies that an illicit bodily union is incompatible with the spiritual union of the disciple with Christ. Taking the 'one flesh' of Gen. 2. 24 to refer specifically to sexual intercourse,[1] he draws an analogy between the bodily union effected in this way and the spiritual union which is established by membership in Christ. These two forms of union cannot co-exist (contrary to what is claimed), because body and spirit need to be in harmony (the body being, indeed, 'a temple of the Holy Spirit within you', verse 19). This is why union with a harlot is so dangerous. Of course, where couples are married 'in the Lord' (as Paul would say) no such danger exists, as the bodily union is then perfectly compatible with the spiritual union which characterises membership in Christ.

From this discussion it may be concluded that Paul's overriding concern is for the maintenance of union with Christ. This is the condition of resurrection life. Legitimate sexual relations do not interfere with this, even if Paul is a little uncertain whether they are positively helpful rather than somewhat distracting (I Cor. 7. 35).

[1]As in some rabbinic texts. It is a mistake to see a distinction between *sōma* and *sarx* in this passage, as if 'body' meant 'the whole man' and 'flesh' meant 'the whole man perverted', while 'spirit' means 'the whole man directed towards God'. Paul here contrasts 'body' and 'spirit' as two different parts of a man which need to be in harmony, and 'flesh' is used as a synonym of 'body' because it is the word that happens to be used in the quotation.

152

(c) *Ephesians 5. 22-33*
The evidence of I Corinthians inevitably leaves a rather negative impression of Paul's attitude to marriage. We get something more positive, however, in his brief instruction to husbands and wives in Colossians 3. 18-19 (see below). We may also note his beautiful use of bridal imagery in II Cor. 11. 2: 'I betrothed you to Christ to present you as a pure bride to her one husband'.

These two passages pave the way for consideration of Eph. 5. 22-33 a passage of outstanding importance. The Epistle to the Ephesians is held by many scholars to be not by Paul himself, but by a later writer, who is inspired by his teaching and writes in his name. But doubt about authorship in no way reduces the value of this epistle for understanding the meaning of marriage in Pauline Christianity. In what follows the writer will be referred to as 'the author', but this is not intended to prejudge the question of authorship.

The author seeks to promote the highest view of marriage as a loving relationship, using the analogy of Christ and the Church. Here we have positive thinking about the nature of marriage itself, not interfered with by any expressions of a preference for celibacy. Stable families are presupposed. The question of divorce and remarriage does not enter the discussion. The author is not dealing with specific problems requiring new decisions, as Paul had to do in I Corinthians. He is simply expanding the exhortation to husbands and wives in a conventional list of messages to the various members of a family (the *Haustafeln*). In a similar, but much briefer, list in Colossians Paul had counselled wives to be subject to their husbands (according to the universally accepted standard of the time with regard to the position of women), and husbands to love their wives (Col. 3. 18-19). The author of Ephesians, who (if he was not Paul himself) was probably directly dependent on Colossians, takes up both these points, and gives them much greater depth and importance by means of a powerful Christological analogy. The relations between husband and wife are elucidated by comparison with the relations between Christ and the Church.

Thus the obedience of wives is recommended as an expression of the obedience which is incumbent upon *all* Christians in their relation to Christ (verses 22-24, *cf.* verse 21). Just as the husband is the 'head' (*kephalē*, a well known Greek usage for 'master') of the wife, so Christ is the head of the Church (verse 23). Having stated the analogy, the author then significantly reverses it: wives are to be subject to their

153

husbands *because* Christ is the head of the Church. They are not, then, to model their behaviour on the example of other wives, even such illustrious wives as Sarah and Rebecca, who were held up as models in Jewish moral exhortation. Rather they are to model their behaviour on the example of the Church, applying to their married life the qualities which are required of all Christians in their obedience to Christ. It will be seen that this adds great moral and emotional force to what is in fact a conventional position.

Husbands, however, have no such customary obligation, so that the section dealing with them needs to be more fully argued. The love of a man for his wife is not a consequence of his marital status, but a matter of choice (it is presupposed that only those aspects of love which are under the control of the will are under discussion). Here the author commands it, but not because of the nature of the marriage bond as such, but directly as a consequence of his analogy of Christ and the Church (verse 25). Christ's love for the Church has been demonstrated in his sacrificial death (*cf.* 1. 7; 5. 2). For his present purpose the author expresses the efficacy of Christ's sacrifice by means of bridal imagery. It corresponds with the ceremonial washing of the bride before the espousals.[1] The distinction between the redemption (verse 26) and the consummation (verse 27) may be intended to reflect the distinction between betrothal and marriage according to Jewish marriage customs. As Christian baptism is also a washing, whereby people are brought into the scope of Christ's redemptive work, there is an implied appeal to discipleship here: the man who is to love his wife knows himself to be loved by Christ. The sacrificial language takes the analogy beyond what actually happens in marriage. Christ's sacrifice, it is true, makes the Church capable of becoming a spotless sacrificial victim, and the washing of baptism effects this in the individual sacramentally. But a husband does not in fact perform the washing and the clothing of the bride. The analogy is true only inasmuch as the husband's love through the course of life, long after the bridal ceremonies have been completed, can have an analogous effect upon his wife in the long term.

The terms of the analogy keep shifting. In verse 27 the Church has ceased to be a fresh young bride, newly washed and clothed, and become a spotless sacrificial victim. At verse 28, where the author reverts to direct exhortation so as to make the practical application of

---

[1]Here the author may be dependent on II Cor. 11. 2, where Paul described his own evangelistic work as the washing of the bride.

the analogy, the Church becomes the body of which Christ is the head (verse 29), and so husbands are bidden to love their wives as their own bodies. Thus the care which Christ has bestowed on the Church is the model for a husband's care for his wife, and this can now be put more simply in terms of the care which a person naturally bestows upon his own physical well-being. This is expressed as self-love, but must surely be intended to mean something akin to the instinct of self-preservation.

It is at this point, with the body analogy before him, that the author quotes the fundamental Jewish text for marriage, Gen. 2. 24. Coming as it does as a comment on the comparison between a man's love of his wife and his love for his body, which has its true analogy in Christ's love of the church, this text concerning the one-flesh union functions as a scriptural warrant for the author's main point, that a man should love his wife as much as he instinctively loves himself. He realises, however, that in using the quotation in this way he is passing beyond the generally accepted meaning of it. So he hastens to point out that the real basis of his thought is the relationship between Christ and the Church (verse 32). Consequently he explains that the text is prophetic. Besides the literal meaning of the text, referring to the union of marriage in general, it expresses God's hidden purpose ('mystery') in a deeper sense (for this interpretation of *mysterion* see further below). That is to unite all men in Christ (*cf.* 1. 9-10), and it is in this sense that the text speaks of Christ and the Church.

Finally, not wishing to enlarge further on the allegorical aspects of his theme, the author briefly summarises the essential moral points which he has made, first with regard to husbands and then with regard to wives (verse 33).

The great value of this passage is the force of its moral appeal. Paul had doubted whether the 'worldly' institution of marriage could really be helpful in relation to the 'spiritual' institution of union with Christ. Here the author makes the spiritual union the model for the marriage relationship, thus supplying a new incentive for Christians to make the best of their marriages, and indeed enriching and ennobling the whole idea of marriage. Paul was motivated, to some extent at least, by the sense that the time was short before the transition to heavenly existence. Here the author has accepted the fact that the end of the age is not really in sight, so that he concentrates on the anticipations of the coming era that are available to Christians in their present existence. Consequently the worldly condition of marriage is the arena for the exercise of spiritual gifts which belong to the coming age. He thereby produces the nearest thing to a Christian theology of marriage to be found in the New Testament.

Three further points must claim our attention. In the first place it is significant that the author's teaching presupposes the normal convention of the day, that a husband can exact the obedience of his wife as of right, whereas a wife has no rights against her husband. The author redresses the balance, not by disputing the convention, but by laying on the husband the moral obligation of self-sacrifice.

Some would argue that the difference here taken for granted is more than a reflection of the contemporary social structure and attitudes towards the sexes, and should be considered an indispensable feature of a Christian doctrine of marriage. From this point of view the passage illustrates the complementarity of the sexes as opposed to their equality. The traditional promise of the bride to obey and of the bridegroom to give bodily respect to his wife may be justified on these grounds. Others would point out that the author's acceptance of contemporary social structures is independent of the theological implications of the passage, and cannot be regarded as morally binding upon the present generation, in which there is a very different structure of personal relationships. From this point of view the passage must be applied to the present situation, in which the equality of husband and wife is generally accepted. This has the advantage of applying to both partners the immensely appealing analogy which is applied only to husbands in verses 25-33.

Secondly, the passage has been taken to constitute an argument for the essential indissolubility of marriage. Seeing that the author works from the relationship of Christ and the Church to that of husband and wife, the basis of the analogy is a union that can never be dissolved, for what Christ has done for his bride can never be undone. The union of Christ and the Church has been established for all time as a result of the redemptive acts of his death and resurrection and exaltation. Similarly the union of husband and wife cannot be undone.

The argument looks plausible, but breaks down on closer examination. The analogy is between the once-for-all acts by which Jesus established his relationship with the Church (potentially all mankind) and the ongoing, repeated behaviour of husbands throughout a lifetime. No analogy is drawn between the event of redemption and the actual marriage ceremony. On the contrary a further analogy is drawn between Christ's continuing care for the

Church and a husband's continuing care for his wife, and the quotation from Gen. 2. 24 is adduced to show how the union of husband and wife so achieved is comparable to the accomplishment of God's purpose to unite all men in Christ. This refers to the actual achievement of union in the married life, not to a hidden union which is supposed to exist when the marriage has failed. It is precisely in order to bring the strongest moral pressure to bear upon couples to prevent their marriages from failing that the author makes use of his involved analogy.

Thirdly, the sacramental character of the marriage ceremony has been deduced from the author's comment on Gen. 2. 24. The marriage union is formed by an outward act, such as the exchange of vows and clasping of hands with lifelong intention. On a sacramental view this outward act is accompanied by a hidden infusion of divine grace to enable the couple to keep their bond. Thus the status of the couple as married persons is validated in heaven, and no earthly dissolution can alter it. This view does not necessarily derive from Ephesians, but there is no doubt that those who hold it have always claimed to be able to deduce it from this epistle.

It is not our purpose here to argue whether this view, which was propounded by the schoolmen in the middle ages, is good theology. Nor do we wish to question whether it applies only to the baptised who are in the covenant of divine grace (as maintained by the Roman Catholic Church), or applies to every monogamous marriage contracted legally with lifelong intention (the position of most Anglicans today who hold the sacramental view). We are here only concerned whether it is a biblical view.

The question turns on the meaning of Eph. 5. 32. After quoting Gen. 2. 24 in the preceding verse, the author says: 'This is a great mystery, and I take it to mean Christ and the church'. The first words are in the Greek *to mysterion touto mega estin,* but the Vulgate translation reads *sacramentum hoc magnum est,* and this was taken to mean 'this sacrament is great'.

It can be said at once that this is a misunderstanding of the meaning of *sacramentum,* due to the later scholastic usage of the word. The Old Latin version probably originally had *mysterium,* but *sacramentum* is found in some Old Latin texts, and is attested in reference to this passage in Latin writers as early as Tertullian (died 220 A.D.). In classical Latin *sacramentum* was a technical term for a sum of money deposited in a law-suit, which (if forfeited) was used for sacred purposes. As a military term it was applied to the contract of enlistment in the army, and so became associated with the military oath. In this way it acquired a more general use for any oath or solemn undertaking. It could thus be used to refer to the plan of God, which is his sacred undertaking, kept secret from men until he puts it into effect. It is used, for instance, of the secret of a king in Tobit 12. 7 (Greek *mystērion*, Vulgate *sacramentum*), and of God's hidden plan in Daniel 4. 9 (Aramaic *rāz*, Greek *mystērion*, Vulgate *sacramentum*).

This is in fact what *mystērion* means in Eph. 5. 32. The basic meaning of this Greek word is 'secret', and in New Testament times it was applied to the secret teachings of religious sects (the mystery religions). In the New Testament itself the word usually refers in some way to God's hidden truth. In Ephesians it is used for God's foreordained plan of redemption (1. 9), especially for the great truth revealed to Paul (3. 1-5) that the Gentiles should be sharers in Christ (3. 6-9). This also seems to be what is meant in 6. 19, the only other occasion when *mystērion* is used in Ephesians. There is thus everything to be said for the view that in 5. 32 it not only refers to God's hidden plan, but also specifically to the inclusion of the Gentiles in Christ, which is the most important feature of it from the author's point of view. Thus the text of Gen. 2. 24, quoted in verse 31, is to his mind a secret, almost a riddle, of the truth that is most important to him (for 'great' = 'important' *cf.* I Tim. 3. 16). The text is, then, an allegory. It speaks of the union of man and wife, but it refers allegorically to the opening of the Church to the Gentiles. When a man takes a wife, his action is symbolic of Christ's taking of the whole Church (of course including the Gentiles) as his bride.

But this is not merely a matter of allegory. For to our author the application to Christ and the Church is the true meaning of the actual text in Genesis. This accords with the general attitude to scriptural interpretation in New Testament times. All scripture is deemed to be prophetic of the end time, when the hidden plan of God is put into effect.[1] Hence Gen. 2. 24 is not simply taken here from its general use in Jewish teaching about marriage. Being a text of scripture, its proper point of reference is the end time, which the primitive church connected with the Christ-event. From this point of view the words of this scripture, which do indeed refer to marriage in the first instance,

---

[1]There is a close parallel to this eschatological interpretation of scripture in the Dead Sea Scrolls. The men of Qumran believed that God's secrets (*rāz*) would be fulfilled in their own time.

reach their true point of reference in relation to God's hidden plan for mankind only when they are applied to Christ. His taking of the Gentiles into the people of God, as a husband takes his bride, is the 'secret', which has been declared mysteriously in the Genesis text, but has had to wait for the time of his revealing to be put into effect.

It now becomes clear why, in the whole of the passage, the true nature of the married relationship is deduced from the relationship of Christ and the Church, and not the other way round. In fact the relationship of Christ and the Church is the theme of the entire epistle, and it is consistent with this that the author uses the symbolism of the Church as the bride of Christ when he gives practical advice to wives and husbands.[1]

It should now also be clear that the Latin *sacramentum* is a perfectly correct translation of *mysterion* in its proper sense of 'secret'. It does not mean 'sacrament' in the modern sense, and only acquired this meaning on account of later developments of Latin theology.

CONCLUSIONS

1.   The ethical teaching of Jesus is concerned with the attitudes and behaviour which fit people for the kingdom of God. His teaching on purity of heart makes even the lustful glance morally equivalent to the act of adultery. His teaching on divorce shows that he was known to be strongly opposed to it, even to the point of declaring the remarried person to be an adulterer. The dispute with the Pharisees gives the legal justification of this position. The primary will of God is that marriage should be permanent, as stated in Gen. 1.27 and 2. 24, and the law of Deut. 24. 1 permitting divorce is only concessionary. Thus those who seek to be fit for God's kingdom will carry through his primary intention and maintain lifelong fidelity. In the conditions of the coming kingdom the institution of marriage will be both fulfilled and transcended in the new spiritual structure of personal relations which belongs to the resurrection life. To this end some are called to celibacy, especially those who are dedicated to the work of the gospel.

2.   The question whether Jesus intended to rescind the legal provision for divorce cannot be decided on the evidence of the relevant passages alone, but depends upon wider considerations concerning the foundation of the Church. If he intended the disciples to be a distinct sect, with its own laws embodying his ideals, it can be argued

---

[1]Paul uses the same imagery in II Cor. 11. 2. It has, of course, precedents in the theme of Israel as God's bride in the Old Testament and is taken up in Rev. 19. 7-8; 21. 2.

that he expressly excluded divorce, which is thus to be regarded as illegal from the very beginning. This is in effect the traditional view. If, on the other hand, the disciples in the period of the ministry are the company of those who accept his teaching and strive to live by it, but without a formal structure and a new body of laws, then his strictures against divorce are an appeal to the conscience and depend for their effect upon personal response. In this case the law of Deut. 24. 1 is not rescinded, but the disciples endeavour to maintain such high ethical standards that they never resort to it. But it is at least conceivable, on this view, that there might be cases of divorce under the Jewish law which Jesus would approve.

3.   However that may be, the evidence of Paul shows that the Church, constituted as a distinct sect in the era after the resurrection, regarded divorce as forbidden by command of the Lord within its own membership. Paul's phrases ('give charge', *parangello;* 'command', *epitage*) suggest that the keeping of this rule depends upon the profound sense of moral authority attaching to the tradition of the words of Jesus rather than upon a legal structure that can be enforced. Christians who have been divorced before their conversion, or whose conversion results in the necessity of divorce, are apparently free to be remarried, though the position is not completely clear. Nothing is said about Christians who do in fact divorce and remarry after their conversion, though the divorced wife is told to remain single (I Cor. 7. 11).

4.   The Matthaean exception in Matt. 5. 32 and 19. 9, however it is to be interpreted, indicates that the saying of Jesus against divorce is treated as law in the Matthaean church. On the traditional interpretation (*porneia* = act of adultery) divorce is permitted in a case of adultery in accordance with a strict application of the Jewish law. Other interpretations make the grounds for divorce only such factors as we would today regard as grounds for nullity.

5.   Both Jesus and Paul accept the normal legal position that a marriage is ended by the death of one of the partners.

6.   Both Jesus and Paul regard the present as the time of preparation for the coming kingdom, when the structure of personal relationships will be transformed. This is the proper explanation of Paul's great emphasis on celibacy and apparent devaluation of marriage. In fact Paul resists those who attempt to forbid marriage, and encourages

husbands and wives to care for one another and to give each other their conjugal rights.

7. Paul's 'other-worldliness' does not affect his moral attitude towards the 'this-worldly' activity of sex. Illicit sexual relations are incompatible with spiritual union with Christ (I Cor. 6. 16-20). Paul thinks that sexual relations within marriage may be somewhat distracting from the primary aim of promoting spiritual union with Christ, but he does not suggest that they are morally incompatible.

8. A much more positive view of marriage is put forward in Eph. 5. 22-33. Here the spiritual union between Christ and the Church is declared to be the reality (though revealed late in time) from which the institution of marriage, as divinely ordained in Gen. 2. 24, is derived. From it the author deduces the qualities which make a true marriage, and thereby enriches the concept of the marriage relationship for what it is in itself. The passage presupposes the permanence of marriage, but does not suggest that marriage is intrinsically indissoluble. This can be read out of the passage only by pressing the analogy further than is actually done by the author. Also the passage does not state that marriage is a sacrament in the modern sense, which depends on a false idea of the meaning of Latin *sacramentum*.

9. Finally, other New Testament passages which have not been considered in this study (I Thess. 4. 3-5; I Tim. 5. 11-14; Titus 2. 1-5; Heb. 13. 4; I Peter 3. 1-7) do not add any further information. They reflect the early church's concern for the avoidance of adultery and for stable marriages, and accept the subordinate position of women without question.

5
A Suggested Diocesan Procedure

If the General Synod were to decide that permission could be given for some divorced persons to be married in church, the following might provide the basis for an agreed procedure. If it, or something like it, were adopted, it would need to be incorporated in Regulations of the General Synod replacing the Regulations of Convocation of 1957.

The procedure would operate pastorally and not juridically: there is no suggestion of courts or tribunals. What is proposed is a procedure by which an incumbent who has been asked to solemnise the marriage of a divorced person informs his bishop of the circumstances and seeks his direction. The bishop and the priest would be taking counsel together about the wisdom of varying in a particular case the Church's normal practice of not solemnising the marriage of divorced persons. Applications for permission for a divorced person to be married in church would therefore always be made by the priest, and not by the couple proposing to marry.

The bishop might deal with cases himself, or delegate some or all of his responsibilities in this matter to a panel of advisers. In the latter eventuality it would be usual for at least one of the advisers to meet the couple wishing to marry, and for that person to consult with the other members of the panel before a decision was reached.

An incumbent would be expected to forward to the bishop every application for remarriage in church and to indicate to the bishop his own recommendation in relation to the application. No incumbent might solemnise the marriage of a divorced person without consulting his bishop according to this procedure; and where the bishop refused an application the incumbent would be expected to abide by that decision.

It would be necessary for the House of Bishops to work out an agreed approach to the implementation of this procedure. For example where the two persons wishing to marry lived in different dioceses they would be free to apply through their respective incumbents to two bishops. The bishops would in such circumstances need to be agreed how the applications were to be regarded.

DRAFT REGULATIONS CONCERNING THE SOLEMNISATION OF MARRIAGE OF A DIVORCED PERSON DURING THE LIFETIME OF A FORMER PARTNER

1. It is not normally the practice of the Church of England to solemnise the marriage of anyone who has been divorced and has a former partner still living.

2. Special permission for the solemnisation of a marriage of a divorced person in these circumstances may be given when the incumbent can give adequate assurances to the bishop that:

(a) the divorced person shows evidence of insight into the causes of the breakdown of the previous marriage, acknowledges with penitence whatever responsibility may have been his for that breakdown, seeks the forgiveness of God and is forgiving himself and intends to make new vows in confidence in God's promises of renewal;

(b) reasonable provision has been made for the spouse and children of the former marriage and that any court order relating to custody or the disposal of property has been complied with;

(c) the couple requesting marriage in church have in their discussion with the incumbent shown understanding of and commitment to the Christian doctrine and practice of marriage and in particular the lifelong character of the marriage;

(d) the couple recognise the binding nature of the marriage vows and intend with God's help to abide by them.

3. Application for permission for a divorced person to be married in church shall be made to the bishop: provided that no application shall normally be considered within a year of the decree absolute being pronounced.

4. Where such a marriage is desired the following procedure shall apply:

(a) Every application for permission shall be made to the bishop by the incumbent of the parish in which at least one of the partners normally resides, and shall be signed by the incumbent. Where it is proposed that the marriage be solemnised by a minister other than the incumbent, that minister shall counter-sign the application.

(b) The incumbent shall indicate to the bishop in writing whether in his judgement the application should be approved, and his reasons therefor.

(c) The bishop shall consider every such application, see the couple, and at his sole discretion approve or refuse the application.

(d) If permission is granted for such a marriage the bishop shall indicate his approval in writing, and shall instruct his registrar to issue a licence for the marriage. If permission is not granted notice of refusal shall be given in writing to the incumbent who shall inform the couple.

5. Any incumbent making application for the bishop's permission for such a marriage shall in his application include the following:

(a) the date of any previous marriage of either of the partners;

(b) the dates of birth of children of any previous marriage, and their present circumstances;

(c) copies of the decree nisi and the decree absolute;

(d) whether either partner has made application through another incumbent for permission for the marriage to be solemnised in church, and, if so, whether and by whom the application was refused; and whether either partner is making a simultaneous application to another bishop;

(e) how long he has known the couple; whether they are regular churchgoers and, if so, of which church; whether there are particular reasons for the application; and any other relevant information.

6. The bishop shall normally notify the former partner of any divorced person seeking permission for remarriage in church of that person's intentions to remarry, unless the couple or the incumbent indicate strong personal reasons why this should not be done.

7. Any incumbent shall be entitled to refuse to solemnise the marriage of a divorced person and to refuse the use of his church for the marriage. Where the partners live in different parishes, and both incumbents refuse to allow the use of their church, the couple may apply for an archbishop's licence to be married in another church.

8.   If the parties to an intended marriage reside in different dioceses, a bishop refusing an application shall notify the bishop of the other diocese.

9.   The bishop may, in consultation with the Bishop's Council, delegate any or all of his powers in this regard to a panel of advisers appointed by him, and in such event an application to the panel shall be deemed for the purposes of these regulations to be an application to the bishop. The bishop may at any time vary or revoke the powers and duties of the panel.

6
Two Examples of Work with Married Couples

. 1. MARRIAGE EDUCATION—A 'WORKSHOP APPROACH'
(A brief account of weekends for couples run by Pauline and Colin Davison for the Church of England Board of Education.)
Has marriage a future or is it crumbling as a basic institution of society? Certainly the divorce figures would suggest that more and more couples are becoming disenchanted with each other and splitting up. On the other hand people are still getting married and trying to make it work. We believe that we are witnessing an expansion of marriage as an institution, that marriage has a bright future but that the word 'marriage' will be used to denote a wider range of options for people who wish to live together and share themselves in a primary relationship.

Workshop method
The 'workshops' for couples which we, through the Church of England Board of Education, have been running for the past three years, have been designed to enable those who are married to explore their relationship with each other, to look at the options they have for enriching it, and to practise using various 'tools' for maintaining themselves.

That is the idea behind the use of the word 'workshops' to describe the weekends when upwards of twelve couples take time off from work, chores, home commitments, etc. and go away to spend time together. A workshop is a place for creating things, for repairing things, borrowing and using tools, exploring and enjoying. So on the weekend couples will practise some of their skills in communicating in fresh ways, making decisions, listening, playing, drawing, imagining, moving. Often people claim to have no such skills and feel that they have to rely on others to do things for them. We seek to affirm people so that they rediscover their capacities and take more and more charge of their own lives and the life of the marriage.

Sickness

Most of the resources of church and society are mobilised to deal with the distresses of marriage, trying to heal the breaches and binding up the wounds. All this work is of great importance but it has one pitfall and that is that marriages have to proclaim themselves 'sick' or near 'breakdown' before anything can be done. We wish to go one step further back and build up in people the capacity to look at the process of their own lives, and to value their own particular way of being married. We want to examine the 'here-and-now' of our relationships, to feel the delight and pain of choice, to decide on the 'will be' for ourselves.

Growth

We think that the churches are in a unique position to provide contexts for couples to grow in. We are not in a position to provide advice or solutions about how marriage ought to be. 'Preparation for marriage' is of course largely nonsense, as it presupposes that somebody knows the situation into which a couple will fit. We don't know how marriage ought to be. We can, however, provide a safe place in which engaged couples can examine their actual relationships, and make their own choices and set their own style.

People who have lived together for some time grow and change, sometimes at different rates. They need to update their contracts, to make space for themselves to grow individually and together.

What happens on a 'workshop'

Up to twelve couples, of any description, married or not, of any age, who regard their relationship as basically worthwhile and who have some investment in enriching it, come together for a weekend residentially from Friday to Sunday lunch. Friday evenings are always difficult. People often fear that they are going to be spied on or forced to divulge things or show off. It takes most of the evening to get the message across that the couples are there for themselves, to talk to each other and not to operate as members of a group.

There are three common areas of concern which always seem to come up very early on.

Self-worth

The first is the difficulty that couples have in feeling good about themselves and each other. There is a socially accepted practice of invalidation, 'putting oneself down', avoiding affirmation. Cycles of

167

invalidation seem to abound in close human relationships, and are frequently shrugged off as 'pin-pricks' not worth bothering about. But these pin-pricks, minor hurts, criticisms and 'put-downs' do have a cumulative effect. Each puts on more and more armour to protect from further hurt until both experience increasing deadness and lack of feeling. The relationship becomes boring.

Right from the word go we invite couples to practise and repractise the skill of reversing this cycle and begin to affirm themselves and each other, privately and publicly. In the introductions we will invite people to say what they like about themselves, their spouse and their relationship. Some embarrassment is felt, but that simply arises from the reversal of the cycle.

Communication

After introductions and spelling out the programme, individuals are invited to begin to look at the second area of concern, that of communication. Virginia Satir in her book *Peoplemaking* suggests that human relationships are either toxic or nurturing. Toxic relationships actively sap the life out of human beings and are characterised by disturbed communication and double messages. A style of communication which says one thing in words and another in feeling and expression has the effect of developing an unreal world in which neither partner can be real. Nurturing relationships are characterised by open, clear communication, negotiated and equal contracts, and affirmation. Virginia Satir guesses that 96 per cent of human families are toxic to some degree.

Over the weekend we set up situations in which couples can, if they want to, look at how they are communicating with each other, with word, expression and touch. So on Friday evening we may invite individuals to draw three 'pictures' (a) how I see myself, (b) how I see my partner, (c) how I imagine my partner sees me; then to share these pictures with the partner in the presence of another couple. The presence of the other couple is important. We who 'run' the workshop have some experience of working with couples, but it seems far more important that couples have an opportunity to use the attention and observation of another couple—to ask them 'what do you see us doing? In doing this the couple take charge in setting up the situation in which they can best work. The assumption here is that if they can do it on a weekend, they can set up similar situations at home.

168

Contract

The third concern is with contracts. It seems a very hard legal word and foreign to the intimate warmth of a marriage, but it has its uses. Marriage is a public contract and very little of it is put into print, even small print. Nevertheless implicit in any relationship are a multitude of unspoken and unexpressed assumptions which to a greater or lesser degree constitute 'the marriage'.

It is only when these assumptions are made conscious and articulated that they can be changed or maintained according to choice. The effect of the women's movement in our society is profound and any marriage where the couple are not healthily renegotiating their contract on the basis of voluntary adapting roles, is in for a rough time!

Renewing contracts can be the major work of the workshop. Contracts about time to be alone, to be with children, to go out, to relate others of the opposite sex, to work, to sleep—any area of the relationship which one or other of the couple desires to change—these are 'tools' available at the workshop for making things new.

Saturday is generally spent in pairs, using at times the attention of another couple, sharing how they see the process of their lives and how they want them to be. One particular activity is the opportunity to speak out all the unsaid things. For example one exercise is to look your spouse in the eye and for ten minutes, without interruption, complete the phrase 'I assume you know that . . .'.

Another exercise is to clear out the garbage, to express all the resentments that have mounted up—again taking time without interruption.

Another is to express everything people can think of in appreciation of their partner. Again and again, the words of love and valuing remain unsaid and taken for granted. Here we reverse the cycle and say them out uninterruptedly. It is important that the partner should attend and not talk. Talking back is a device for blocking the process and keeping things as they were. That's why things get unsaid, no one listens!

Worship

Sunday morning is spent largely in eucharist. Couples at past workshops have designed and participated in extremely imaginative and moving acts of worship. It is always a 'high' time of the weekend and people always look good as well as feel good. They say it's because they have had time for each other, to nurture each other and to listen to each other. They have said things to each other they have never said before, surprised each other afresh with their love and delight.

One couple said recently 'when we left the workshop we talked all night. We have never talked so much before or at such a level'.

2. A MARRIAGE ENRICHMENT GROUP

This is a form of house-group geared to *couples* and to the subject of *marriage*, initiated by Revd. David Tustin of the Diocese of Lichfield.

1. Membership:
   four or five married couples

2. Place:
   home of one participating couple

3. Seating:
   natural fire-side semicircle

4. Programme:
   coffee and biscuits on arrival at 8.00 p.m.
   informal discussion for about two-and-a-half hours
   finally fix date of next meeting

5. Emphasis:
   we try to share experiences rather than abstract opinions

6. Leadership:
   two variant types
   (a) *one experienced couple leads*
   in advance they map out likely agenda
   they decide which of them will watch out for special points
   they facilitate discussion generally
   each co-leader brings out or brings up his/her special points as opportunity occurs
   (b) *fluid leadership*
   this can happen naturally with a more experienced group;
   it presupposes sufficient resources latent in group

7. Resources:

(a) *necessary*

general group leadership skill

someone who has read some key books on this subject

(b) *desirable*

someone with counselling experience

at least one couple who have attended a residential workshop for married couples

8. Strengths:

provides good 'growth group'

facilitates dialogue within each couple

enjoyable, helpful, easy and informal

arouses interest to read and discuss further

enables couples to share difficulties and solutions

9. Weaknesses:

with fluid leadership group can wander

special care needed to integrate new couple into established group

10. Key books:

D. & V. Mace, *We can have better marriages* (Oliphant, 60p)

Eric Berne, *Games People Play* (Penguin, 55p)

J. Dominian, *The Marriage Relationship Today* (M. U., 15p)

J. Dominian, *Christian Marriage* (Darton, Longman and Todd, £1.25)

Anne Townsend, *Marriage without Pretending* (S. U., 80p)

T. A. Harris, *I'm OK—You're OK* (Pan, 75p)

Carl Rogers, *Becoming Partners* (Constable, £1.95)

T. Gordon, *Parent Effectiveness Training* (Plume, £2.95)

V. Satir, *Peoplemaking* (Science & Behaviour, £3.25)

T. Bovet, *Handbook of Marriage* (Longmans; out of print)

11. Typical subject matter:

How are you settling in (for newly weds)? How does *she* find it, working *and* running a home?

Is your marriage a partnership? Did you marry a stranger? How do you handle conflict? Who makes up after a row—is it always the same one? Can you say what you really think and *feel?* Common policy over money, sex, children, in-laws, friends and outside activities.

What do you most appreciate/ resent about your partner? How far are mutual expectations expressed/ fulfilled, etc.?

7
The Law of Divorce

In Chapter 2 of our report we describe the salient features of the English law on marriage and divorce. The changes in the law of divorce made in 1969 were undoubtedly significant, but they represent only the latest stage in a process of development which has been going on over hundreds of years. In the first part of this appendix we give a brief account of the evolution of the jurisdiction to separate spouses and to dissolve marriages, and indicate the close involvement of the Church in these matters in every period. In the second part we describe in greater detail the working of the present law on divorce.

THE EVOLUTION OF THE MATRIMONIAL JURISDICTION

Ecclesiastical courts were separated from lay courts in the reign of William the Conqueror and shortly afterwards acquired sole jurisdiction over matrimonial matters. This jurisdiction they retained until 1857 when it was removed from them entirely by the Matrimonial Causes Act and vested in Her Majesty to be exercised in 'the Court for Divorce and Matrimonial Causes'. For hundreds of years, therefore, the Church had complete control over the administration of the law of marriage. The doctrine of indissolubility of the marriage bond prevailed. A marriage could be brought to an end by the ecclesiastical courts by means of a decree of nullity. The divorce *a mensa et thoro* (from home and hearth) was not however a divorce in the modern sense but only a legal separation, because it did not dissolve the marriage nor enable the parties subsequently to remarry.

At the Reformation, the Church in England did not accept the general approach adopted by Reformers on the Continent who took the view that divorce *a vinculo* (i.e. divorce in the modern sense) for adultery should be permitted on the basis of Jesus' teaching recorded by Matthew, and that divorce for 'malicious desertion' was justified by reference to I Corinthians 7. 15 and I Timothy 5. 8. A proposed code of Canons known as the *Reformatio legum ecclesiasticarum* was drawn up in England but this had not passed into law by the time of

Edward VI's death, and an attempt to revive it under Elizabeth I proved abortive. If passed it would have allowed divorce *a vinculo* for adultery, desertion, 'deadly hostility' and prolonged ill-treatment of a wife by a husband.

The Canons of 1597 relating to marriage, incorporated into the Canons of 1604, provided only for the annulling of 'pretended marriages' and for divorce *a mensa et thoro*. There is however evidence that a certain number of second marriages after divorce did take place in the latter half of the sixteenth century and later; these were justified by reference to the view held by many churchmen that adultery dissolved the marriage bond.

During the seventeenth century Anglican divines were divided in their views as to the lawfulness of divorce *a vinculo*. Some thought marriage indissoluble, others thought the teaching of Christ allowed divorce for adultery, a few held that desertion as well as adultery justified divorce. Bishop John Cosin for example held that the reality of marriage consisted in the personal relationship of husband and wife, so that separation 'from bed and board' was itself a breach of the marriage bond. Bishop Cosin argued at length from scripture, the Fathers and the Reformation divines that the innocent party to divorce might marry again. He described his opponents' emphasis on the breach occasioned by remarriage as 'chimeral and fancy'.[1] In 1670 he supported a Bill which enabled Lord Roos to remarry during the lifetime of his wife against whom the Ecclesiastical Court had granted a decree *a mensa et thoro* on the ground of her adultery. The Bill passed, and became a precedent which was followed with increasing frequency, until by the passing of the Matrimonial Causes Act 1857 a total of 317 private acts had passed, with little if any opposition from the Church.

The Matrimonial Causes Act 1857 followed the report of a Royal Commission. Like all subsequent divorce legislation, it was in part the product of popular demand and pressure. The right to remarry had previously been obtained only by a small number of rich and influential people able to pay for private Acts of Parliament. The Act of 1857 extended the right of everyone who could obtain a divorce on one of the grounds specified in the Act, namely:

   (a) in a husband's petition—adultery;

   (b) in a wife's petition—incestuous adultery or bigamy with

---

[1]Cosin, *Works* (LACT), IV, p. 492.

adultery or adultery coupled with cruelty, or adultery coupled with desertion without reasonable excuse for two years or upwards.

Churchmen were divided in their response to the Act. Some were able to accept it because its provisions were within the terms of the Matthaean exception.[1] Religious opposition to the Act included those who were totally opposed to divorce, and also those who disliked the Act because it permitted remarriage of the guilty party. The Act was of major significance in removing jurisdiction over marriage from the ecclesiastical courts to the civil courts and in making divorce available much more widely. 1857 marks the beginning of the development of a legal response to marriage breakdown, a development which is still continuing.

Because the Act made it lawful for the parties to remarry after a divorce 'as if the prior marriage had been dissolved by death' (s. 57), it was necessary to provide for the position of the clergyman who objected on theological grounds to solemnising the marriage of a divorced person who was otherwise qualified to be married in church. The Act therefore enacted that no clergyman was to be 'liable to any suit, penalty or censure for solemnising or refusing to solemnise the marriage of any such person'. Although a clergyman might himself refuse to solemnise such a marriage he was, however, obliged by law to 'permit any other minister in Holy Orders of the said United Church [of England and Ireland] entitled to officiate within the diocese in which such church or chapel is situate, to perform such marriage service in such church or chapel' (s. 58). These provisions remained on the statute book in this form until 1937, and afforded considerable scope for dissension between clergy.

After 1857 the number of divorces grew slowly, but there is nothing to show that this was due to the increased availability of divorce as opposed to changes going on in society.

A Royal Commission reporting in 1912 recommended a number of reforms which would have the effect of widening the grounds for divorce. After a number of unsuccessful attempts by Parliament to enact these reforms, which were in general opposed by the Church, a Bill sponsored by Mr. A. P. Herbert (subsequently Sir Alan Herbert), became law as the Matrimonial Causes Act 1937. By this Act the grounds for divorce were extended to include cruelty, desertion for

---

[1]See Chapter 3, paras.. 107-109, 119.

three years, and incurable insanity, as well as the existing ground of adultery. Wilful refusal became a ground for annulling a marriage (in addition to incapacity), such a marriage being voidable as opposed to void *ab initio*. These provisions formed the basis of the divorce jurisdiction of the courts until the Divorce Reform Act 1969 came into force on 1st January 1971.

At the same time, the objectionable provision originally enacted in s. 58 of the Matrimonial Causes Act 1857 was repealed and it was provided that:

> 'No clergyman of the Church of England or of the Church in Wales shall be compelled to solemnise the marriage of any person whose former marriage has been dissolved on any ground and whose former husband or wife is still living or to permit the marriage of any such person in the church or chapel of which he is the minister' (s. 12).

Despite subsequent changes in the law of divorce, this provision has been re-enacted and remains the law at the present day (see now Matrimonial Causes Act 1965, s. 8(2), replacing Matrimonial Causes Act 1950, s. 13(2)). The corollary to it is that a Church of England clergyman may legally solemnise the marriage of a divorced person notwithstanding that Resolutions of the Convocations have urged clergy not to avail themselves of this right.

THE PRESENT LAW OF DIVORCE

The Matrimonial Causes Act 1973, which came into operation on the 1st January 1974, consolidated various enactments relating to matrimonial proceedings, including the whole of the Divorce Reform Act 1969 and the whole of the Nullity of Marriage Act 1971. It contains the principal provisions relating to dissolution and annulment of marriages and judicial separation, and also sections dealing with the financial relief available to parties to a marriage and children of the family. The Act, together with rules made pursuant to the Act, constitutes the basic code of divorce law and practice at the present time.

Restrictions on petitions for divorce

Successive statutes have contained a prohibition against presentation to the court of a petition for divorce within three years from the date of the marriage (s. 1(i) of Matrimonial Causes Act 1937, s. 2 of

Matrimonial Causes Act 1950, s. 2 of Matrimonial Causes Act 1965 and s. 3 of Matrimonial Causes Act 1973). Such a petition can only be presented with leave of the court if the judge is satisfied that the case is one of exceptional hardship suffered by the petitioner, or of exceptional depravity on the part of the respondent. It is not sufficient to prove merely that the marriage has broken down irretrievably. The court has to make a provisional finding of fact that the case is one of exceptional hardship or exceptional depravity. This restriction has the same effect as it has always had of limiting the number of cases where divorce proceedings can be commenced within a short time after the marriage. The retention of the restriction accords with the recommendation of the Archbishop's Group on the law of divorce in their Report *Putting Asunder*.[1]

In considering an application for leave to present a petition within three years of the date of the marriage the judge is required to have regard to the interests of any child of the family and to the question whether there is reasonable probability of a reconciliation between the parties during the three year period (s. 3(2)). In order to encourage reconciliation a practice has been evolved for the High Court and all Divorce County Courts whereby the court can refer the case to the Court Welfare Officer, who will in turn refer the parties to such other persons or bodies as may seem appropriate to assist with the process of conciliation.[2]

Judicial separation

A petition for judicial separation can be presented to the court at any time including within three years of the date of the marriage. Breakdown of the marriage is not the ground for a decree. Any of the facts which can be relied upon in support of an allegation of breakdown of marriage can also be relied upon as a ground for judicial separation. A decree grounded upon any such fact can be treated as sufficient proof in subsequent divorce proceedings of the fact by reference to which it was granted. Thus it is possible for a spouse to obtain a decree of judicial separation within three years of the date of the marriage and a divorce in reliance upon the same fact immediately after the expiry of the three year period. The advantage of being able to seek a decree of judicial separation within the three year period is that the court then has jurisdiction to deal with

---

[1]*Op. cit.*, para. 78.
[2]See Practice Direction (1971) (W.L.R. 223).

questions relating to the financial position of the parties, including property rights (s. 21 *et seq.*). It is in consequence a form of relief sought within the three-year period rather more frequently than in the past. Relief by way of judicial separation was approved by the Archbishop's Group.[1]

Divorce

The only ground for divorce for either party to a marriage is that the marriage has broken down irretrievably (s. 1). There are five facts upon which a petitioner can rely in support of an allegation that the marriage has broken down irretrievably, and the court must be satisfied that one or more of such facts has been proved before it can pronounce a decree. Once such a fact has been proved, however, the court is obliged to grant a decree, unless it is satisfied on all the evidence that the marriage has not broken down irretrievably (s. 1(4)). In practice in the majority of cases the proof of one of the five facts results in the pronouncement of a decree.

The five facts are:

(a) that the respondent has committed adultery and the petitioner finds it intolerable to live with the respondent;

(b) that the respondent has behaved in such a way that the petitioner cannot reasonably be expected to live with the respondent;

(c) that the respondent has deserted the petitioner for a continuous period of at least two years immediately preceding the presentation of the petition;

(d) that the parties to the marriage have lived apart for a continuous period of at least two years immediately preceding the presentation of the petition and the respondent consents to a decree being granted;

(e) that the parties to the marriage have lived apart for a continuous period of at least five years immediately preceding the presentation of the petition.

Adultery

The petitioner must not only prove that the respondent has committed adultery but also that he finds it intolerable to live with the respondent. The intolerability does not have to be in consequence of

[1]*Op. cit.,* para. 38 and Appendix C, para. 4.

the adultery.[1] The adultery may be one matter in a whole history of unkindness and it may occur before or after the parties have separated.

Adultery can be proved in undefended proceedings for divorce by production in evidence of a statement in writing signed by the respondent admitting the adultery. It is then sufficient for the petitioner to identify the respondent's signature and no enquiry agent or other person who took the statement is required to be a witness.[2] This modern practice is simpler and less expensive than that formerly adopted in relation to confessions of adultery. It may at first sight appear to open the door to false evidence, but the evidence of the petitioner has to be taken into account as well as the statement of the respondent and the totality of the evidence must satisfy the court that a finding of adultery can properly be made.

As an incentive towards reconciliation a prospective petitioner has a period of six months within which to decide whether to seek a divorce in reliance upon a particular act or acts of adultery known to the petitioner. If the parties live together in the same household for a period or periods together exceeding six months after discovery of the adultery, then reliance cannot be placed upon that adultery for the purposes of a divorce. Any period or periods less than six months have to be disregarded in determining whether the petitioner finds it intolerable to live with the respondent (s. 2(1), (2) and (6)).

Behaviour

Behaviour covers an infinite range of conduct, both active and passive. It can include behaviour caused by mental or physical illness or injury and be involuntary.[3] In determining whether the petitioner cannot reasonably be expected to live with the respondent the court will have regard to the particular petitioner and the particular respondent and will not apply simply an objective test.[4]

If the parties live together for a period or periods together totalling more than six months from the date of the final incident relied upon by the petitioner and held by the court to support his allegation then that fact has to be taken into account by the court in determining whether the petitioner cannot reasonably be expected to live with the

---

[1] *Cleary v. Cleary* (1974) 1 W.L.R. 73.
[2] See Practice Direction (1973) 1 W.L.R. 1052.
[3] See *Thurlow v. Thurlow* (1975) 3 W.L.R. 161.
[4] See *Ash v. Ash* (1972) Fam. 135.

respondent. As in the case of adultery therefore a petitioner is given a total period of six months for an attempted reconciliation. If the reconciliation lasts for a period in excess of six months then the allegations of behaviour may be treated as too stale to justify a finding in the petitioner's favour.

Desertion

Although the Act refers to a continuous period of two years separation it is possible to add together periods of separation before and after the periods of reconciliation provided there is a total of two years separation within a period of two years and six months immediately preceding the presentation of the petition. This is because no account is to be taken of any period or periods not exceeding six months in all during which the parties lived with each other in the same household (s. 1(5) and (6)). Thus once again a party can attempt a reconciliation without prejudicing his right to seek relief if necessary.

Two years separation

Parties to a marriage are treated as living apart unless they are living with each other in the same household (s. 2(6)). There must be evidence of termination of the consortium, but this can be provided even when the parties are residing under the same roof. The fact that no property adjustment order can take effect until decree absolute (s. 23(3)) means that a dispute about the parties' capital in the matrimonial home cannot be disposed of at an early stage and the parties usually have no other capital to use to rehouse themselves. There is a similar difficulty in relation to local authority housing where no action is taken by the local authority until after decree nisi or decree absolute. Accordingly the number of cases where parties live apart under the same roof for two years and then obtain a 'consent' divorce is tending to increase.

As in the case of desertion the parties are not prejudiced from seeking relief simply because they have attempted a reconciliation. If during a period of two and a half years prior to a petition they have lived together for a period or periods together not exceeding six months they can still rely on a number of periods of separation together totalling two years (s. 2(5)).

Five years separation

The respondent to a petition for divorce based on five years separation may oppose the grant of a decree on the ground that the dissolution of the marriage will result in grave financial or other hardship to him and that it would in all the circumstances be wrong to dissolve the marriage (s. 5(1)). It is not difficult to establish financial hardship, but protection in this respect is afforded by s. 10 which prevents a decree from being made absolute until proper financial provision has been made for the respondent. The number of cases where the financial hardship is grave and cannot be compensated for by financial provision are likely to be minimal. If 'other hardship' is relied upon it must be grave but it can include religious or social degradation if the facts justify such a finding.[1] In practice the number of cases where a respondent resists the granting of a decree are few but financial relief is usually sought as a matter of course. The recommendation of the Archbishop's Group that adequate financial protection should be afforded to a respondent spouse has therefore been put into effect.[2]

Practical operation of the divorce law
The Archbishop's Group emphasised that it was 'implicit in the doctrine of breakdown that a decree of divorce cannot rightly be made while any reasonable hope remains that the parties might be reconciled'.[3] As can be seen from the above account of the main provisions of the Matrimonial Causes Act 1973, the present divorce law has regard to the possibility and desirability of reconciliation. Parties are actively encouraged to become reconciled if they seek a divorce within three years of the date of their marriage and they are given a reasonable time to attempt a reconciliation without being debarred, as happened under the pre-1969 law, from seeking relief in reliance upon, for example, adultery or desertion. Furthermore, solicitors are required to file a certificate with any petition saying whether or not they have discussed the question of reconciliation with the petitioner. The court also has power at any stage of the proceedings for divorce to adjourn the case with a view to attempts being made to effect a reconciliation (s. 6(2)).

While solicitors, barristers, and judges are conscious of the desirability of encouraging reconciliation and can be assumed to do so wherever possible, in the majority of cases the parties themselves have

---

[1]See *Banik v. Banik* (1973) 1 W.L.R. 860 and *Rukat v. Rukat* (1975) 2 W.L.R. 201.
[2]*Op. cit.*, para. 64.
[3]*Op. cit.*, para. 76.

decided that their marriage has broken down before they even consult a solicitor. The number of successful reconciliations attributable to the efforts of lawyers or judges must in consequence be very small.

The Archbishop's Group considered that in no case should agreement of the parties by itself suffice to effect a divorce.[1] The sanction of the court is still required under the present law, but recent changes making divorce available without attendance at court could be said to have affected the popular understanding of the solemnity of a divorce. After 1st December 1975 in any undefended case where there were no children of the family and the petitioner relied on any fact except 'behaviour', a petition for divorce or judicial separation was dealt with upon affidavit evidence and there was no hearing in open court. Since April 1977 this has been extended so that in any undefended case the petition for divorce or judicial separation is dealt with upon affidavit evidence and there is no hearing in open court save in rare cases where some special difficulty arises. The decree is still pronounced by a judge in open court. Questions relating to the arrangements for the care of any children of the family are heard separately by a judge in chambers and not in open court.

---

[1] *Op. cit.*, paras. 48, 59.

8
Oral Evidence given to the Marriage Commission

Mr N. Tyndall on behalf of the National Marriage Guidance Council
The Rev. Dr. E. W. Trueman Dicken
The Rev. Dr. O. O'Donovan
The Bishop of Truro
Canon D. A. J. Stevens
The Bishop of St Albans
Lady Oppenheimer
Monsignor W. A. Purdy
The Rev. Theodore Davey
The Bishop of Southwark
Representatives of the Institute of Marital Studies
Dr. J. Dominian

The Commission extends its grateful thanks to these witnesses, as also to all the many other individuals, groups and bodies who have submitted written evidence for its consideration.